# AMERICAN AMAZONS:

## COLONIAL WOMEN WHO CHANGED HISTORY

(THE GRANDFATHER SERIES #2)

ALEX BUGAEFF

ALSO BY **ALEX BUGAEFF**

*Pilgrims To Patriots, A Grandfather Tells The Story*

(The Grandfather Series, #1)

To

Pinny "Peach" Bugaeff,

Gregor Alexis Bugaeff

And

Samantha Lee Makuch

# CONTENTS

Amazon /a-mə-zon/ n. I. Female warrior of a mythical race; 2. Tall, strong or athletic woman.

# I

## MOLLY PITCHER, REVOLUTIONARY WAR CANNONEER

"**B**OOM!"

I heard it as I stepped from my car in my daughter's driveway. The blast came from the backyard. As I ran in that direction, I heard it again.

"BOOM!"

I kept running until I got a glimpse. Hannah, my 12-year-old granddaughter, stood in a housedress with a long pole in her hand. The pole had a rag wrapped around one end. Close by was a black plastic drainpipe, propped on a log. And most curious was an old boom box portable radio sitting on the ground at her feet. I walked up to her.

"Stand back, Gomps," she ordered. "This cannon is loud!"

With that, she put a beanbag in the pipe and rammed it down with the pole. Next, she put in an old baseball and rammed that down. She stood to one side, bent down, and pressed a button on the boom box.

"BOOM!"

"Hannah, what are you doing?" I asked.

"A reality test," she replied.

"A reality test! What in the world are you testing?"

"Your story about Molly Pitcher. The one you told us last year. It was a good story, but I had a hard time believing that she could have loaded a cannon, so I thought I would try it myself!"

"Well, I'll be darned," I said. "And?"

"She could have done it easily."

Just then, I saw Hannah's mom, Mandy, walking toward us from the house.

"Hi, Dad," she chirped. "I see you've found our Revolutionary War cannoneer."

"I sure have. What's this about?"

"It started with Hannah asking me if we had any of this stuff. We rummaged around in the basement and found it all."

"Then, I found a cannon sound on the 'Net," Hannah said, "and downloaded it onto a CD."

"The hardest part was the dress. I asked Mom if she had some kind of flowing skirt and she came up with this old housedress."

"Mandy, did you know what Hannah was up to?" I asked.

"Oh, I asked her," Mandy replied, "but all she said was, 'You'll see.' I learned long ago not to ask a lot of questions when she gets on a mission.

"By the way, Hannah," I asked, "what's the beanbag for?"

"The gunpowder bag," Hannah replied. "They sewed each load of gunpowder into a cloth bag to make it easier to handle."

"Got it. What's next?"

"Now that I know she could have done it, I want to hear the story again."

"Again? Really?" I asked.

"Yup," she said, "that is such a great story, and you made it sound like we were there. Could you tell it now?"

"Now?"

"I have an idea," Mandy interrupted. "I'm about to get Carter from baseball practice. Why don't you wait until we get back and we can all hear it?"

Carter was Hannah's ten-year-old brother. The previous year, the two had listened to my stories about the nation's Founding.

"Fine by me," I said, "but what about Mark?"

"He went to run errands," Mandy said, "but he should be back before me. I'm sure he'd like to join us."

"Great. Hannah, while we're waiting let's go in and have a snack."

"Sounds good!"

We all gathered on the back deck. Mandy had made some iced tea and we each had a glass.

"You sure you want me to tell the Molly Pitcher story again?" I asked.

"Yup," Hannah and Mandy said, together.

"Carter? You on board?"

"Oh, yeah. I liked that story."

"Mark?" I asked.

"Same here."

"OK. It won't come out exactly the same, but it should be pretty close. Here goes.

❧

"After the Revolutionary War, they called her Molly Pitcher, but her real name was Mary Ludwig. She was born on a Pennsylvania farm in 1754 to German parents. Like all farm children, she did chores around the barn. As she grew bigger and stronger, she carried hay bales and buckets of water.

When she was 13, she married William Hays, a barber."

"I remember your saying that, Gomps" Hannah said. "I couldn't believe she got married that young."

"I remember your surprise, but I think you got used to the idea as we got further into the story. Children grew up faster, married younger, and often died younger, too."

"Yeah," she said, "but I still can't get over that if I lived back then, I might be getting married next year."

"Let's get back to the story," muttered Mark.

"I'm with you," I said. "In 1777, William wanted to help fight the British, so he joined the Continental Army. He was put in an artillery regiment and became an artilleryman."

"I remember," Carter said. "He got to shoot cannons, but what was his job called again?"

"He was a rammer."

"Oh, yeah," Carter continued. "He was the guy with the ramrod. He cleaned the cannon barrel with the rags wrapped around it and loaded the next round. Didn't they call that rag the 'sponge'?"

"That's right, Carter," I said, "Hannah practiced it herself today."

"Yeah, I heard about that," he said. "Hannah, could you do it?"

"I think so. It would depend on how heavy a real ramrod was. I read that rammers didn't have to handle the powder or the cannonballs. They had other guys to do that. Plus, Molly was grown up and stronger than I am. But, yeah, I could."

"I think so, too, Hannah," I said. "Now, back to Molly's story.

"In those days some soldiers' wives got together behind the battle lines to help the troops. They sewed uniforms, did some cooking, and nursed the men if they were sick or wounded. To do that, the wives set up their own camps not far from the troops. When the troops moved, they moved.

"Molly decided to join the wives so she could help William and the other artillerymen. Her camp followed William's regiment from place to place.

"In the winter of 1777-78, the Army set up camp in Valley Forge, Pennsylvania. General George Washington's wife, Martha, was a leader of the wives' group there."

"That surprised me," Carter interrupted. "She could have stayed home."

"She could have, Carter, but not only was she right there, she organized the wives' groups, too."

"Why do you think she did that?" Hannah asked.

"Hannah, it looks like she saw the need, got the idea for the groups and just did it. She talked to the wives of other generals and they followed her lead. Next thing you know, they had it all set up."

"Wasn't it dangerous?" Hannah continued.

"Maybe not from a battle standpoint. I don't think the British would have attacked them — but from a weather and disease standpoint, yes. Their camps were right out in the fields, just like the troops', and if you remember, this was a brutal winter. The troops left bloody footprints in the snow from lack of boots and the women in the camps suffered just as much."

"I remember," Carter said. "What kind of housing did the women have in the camps, Gomps?"

"Tents."

"Brrr," they both said. "They really had to be brave to volunteer for that."

"Last time, you said that Mary probably knew Martha Washington," Hannah said. "Can we find out for sure?"

"Maybe not. We don't have anything from Molly about that, and there's nothing definite from any of Martha's writings. So the only other source would have been her letters with George, but she burned those."

"Burned them?" Carter exclaimed. "Why?"

"She felt that the letters between her and George were no one's business," I said. "She didn't want them to become the stuff of gossip. So after he died, she threw them in the fire."

"Aw, what a waste," Carter observed.

"Yes, it was."

"Now, back to Molly. In the middle of the winter, William's artillery regiment trained at Valley Forge. He practiced with the ramrod and sponge to clean the cannon barrel. He needed lots of water to do that. And since artillery was hot work, even in winter, he and the other artillerymen needed drinking water, too.

"Molly volunteered to break off from her camp duties in order to bring the water to him in buckets. The women who did this were called 'water girls.'

"When spring came, the Army left Valley Forge to take up the fight against the British again. William's regiment fought on one battleground after another. In each battle, Molly and the other water girls were right in the middle of the action, running up to the cannons with their buckets.

"In June, the Continentals fought the British at Monmouth Courthouse, New Jersey. The temperature soared to 100 degrees, and the heat from the cannons made it even hotter. The fighting continued through the day with one side and then the other gaining ground.

"Suddenly, William was hit and went down! Without missing a beat, Molly put down her buckets, grabbed William's ramrod and took over for him. She had seen how to do it in the training at Valley Forge.

"First, the sponge to clean the barrel. Then, the gunpowder – ram it in. Then the hay wad – ram it in. Then the cannonball – ram it in. She stood back, held her ears, and BOOM!

"Molly kept up the firing for the rest of the day. The smoke stung her eyes and the smell of gunpowder burned her nose. Musket shot and cannonballs whistled past her, and one tore right through her petticoat! She wasn't hurt, but part of her skirt was torn away. Still, she kept on firing, and in the end . . . we beat the British."

"Yay!" both kids shouted.

"Ah," I said. "But, remember that this was not the end of the story."

"Oh, yeah," Carter said. "Washington saw her, and . . ."

"Be quiet," Hannah scolded. "I want to hear Gomps tell it."

"OK, go ahead, Gomps."

"During the battle, General Washington had seen Molly firing the cannon. He was so impressed that he made her a sergeant and put her in for a military pension. From then on, everyone called her Sergeant Molly."

"That's so cool, Gomps," exclaimed Hannah. "But I want to hear again how she got the name Molly Pitcher."

"Can't tell the story without that. In those days, Molly was a common nickname for Mary. And 'Pitcher!' was what William and the other artillerymen called out when they needed a drink – a pitcher of water. They yelled, 'Molly, pitcher, pitcher!' At least, that's how the story goes."

"While we're on the subject of stories, Gomps," Hannah began, "when I was browsing for the cannon sound, I found a website that said that this Molly Pitcher story might have been made up. Are you sure it's true?"

"I'm pretty sure. There are a number of reports from people who were there. The best seems to be from Joseph Plumb Martin. He was a Continental soldier who kept a detailed diary of every battle he was in.

"One of those battles was Monmouth Courthouse and Joseph wrote that he had seen Molly firing the cannon and getting her skirt shot away. He quoted her as making a pretty raunchy remark at the time, but I'm not going to tell that."

"Aw, c'mon, Gomps, what'd she say?" Carter pleaded.

"Forget it. When you're old enough, you can read his diary for yourself. It's published."

"Thanks, Dad," said Mandy with a sigh of relief.

"You also can find her pension in the records of Congress and in the Army pay records."

"That's good enough for me," Hannah concluded. "I'm glad it was real. It's good to know that a woman could do that."

"What happened to her?" Carter asked.

"After the war, she moved back to Pennsylvania and had a big family."

"What about William?" Carter asked.

"He went back to Pennsylvania with Molly, and recovered completely. They lived together there until he died in 1786. Soon after, Molly remarried and lived a long time with her second husband. She died in 1832 at about 78 years."

"What a great story," Hannah said. "I could hear that again."

"That's it for now," Mark broke in.

"Just one more thing," I said. "I have a surprise for you."

"You do?" Hannah exclaimed. "I thought that was the end."

"That was the end of the Mary Ludwig Hays story," I said with a wink, "but not of the story of women cannoneers in the Revolutionary War."

"No way!" Carter shouted. "There's more Mollys?"

"You mean cannoneers?"

"Yeah."

"At least one, that we know of," I said.

"Another one was Margaret Corbin, wife of John Corbin. John was an artilleryman in the Continental Army, just like William Hays. He served with the regiment that fought against the British invasion of New York City in 1776."

"*Before* Molly?" the kids chimed.

"That's right," I said. "And Margaret was a water girl just like Mary.

"As the Continentals were pushed back to northern Manhattan, John was hit; but in his case, he died.

"Just like Mary, Margaret took his ramrod and kept up the firing until she herself was hit. She survived, and three years later she was made a captain and given a pension, too. From then on, she was called '*Captain* Molly.'"

"Two Mollys?" Hannah observed skeptically.

"Yup," I said, "remember that this one's name was Margaret, and 'Molly' was a nickname for Margaret, too."

"Aha," Hannah said.

"And *that's* the end of the story," I said.

"Thanks, Gomps," Mark said with a smile.

"Yeah, thanks, Gomps," the kids chimed together.

"Is it really the end?" Mandy asked.

"You never know," I said, smiling.

# 2

## THE FIRST COLONIAL FEMINIST

"Gomps, I have a question," Hannah said.

We were all still sitting on the deck, drinking our iced tea, and I had just finished the story of Molly Pitcher.

"What's that, Hannah?"

"The stories you told last year about how America was formed were almost all about men. I know that they did just about everything, but weren't there women who did things, too?"

"You mean like Molly Pitcher?"

"Yeah, hearing that story again made me wonder."

"You're right, Hannah. Men set up the country — we call it 'Founding'— but there were women who did things, too, a lot more than people know."

"Like Molly?"

"Like Molly and in other ways."

"Could you tell us?"

"Well, I couldn't do it in an hour. There are so many of them that it would take a lot of story times."

"That would be OK with me," Hannah said. "Dad, Mom, could we do something like we did last year?"

"That would be up to Gomps, first," Mark said. "If it's OK with him, I'd just worry about homework getting done. Mandy, what do you think?"

"Same with me," Mandy replied. "Last year's story times really didn't take that long. As long as homework and chores get done, I'm good with it. If it still works, we could have the same schedule.

"How about you, Carter?"

"Sounds boring." Carter said, wrinkling his nose. "You guys go ahead and I'll just do something else."

"You didn't like the Molly Pitcher story?" I asked.

"Oh, I liked that one, but that was just one."

"Suppose I told you that Mary and Margaret were not the only women who fought in battles?" I said.

"I didn't know that, but what else?"

"There were spies, businesswomen, writers, at least one pastor, political leaders, and even a traitor. Women did just about everything that men did, just in different ways, sometimes."

"Well, that sounds pretty good. OK, I'll give it a try."

"Carter, you sound like you're leaving yourself an out," Mandy said. "I think you need to hear all of it."

"Also, Carter, I'll be retelling some of the stories I told last time, like Molly Pitcher," I said. "If I remember right, you were pretty interested in some of them."

"Yeah, I was," Carter said. "OK, I'm in."

"How about Wednesday nights, again?" I asked. "Is there anyone who can't make it?"

No one said a word, so Mandy concluded, "Silence means consent. Can we start this week?"

"Fine by me," I replied. "Incidentally, Mandy, your mother tells some of these stories better than I do. Is it OK if I bring her along for those?"

"Oh, great!" everyone chimed. "We like Peach's stories, too."

It was the next Wednesday evening and I was at the kids' house, as planned. We had finished dinner, so I started right in.

"Tonight, I'm going to tell the story of Anne Hutchinson," I said.

"Anne was born in England in 1591 to Bridget and Francis Marbury. Francis was a minister in the Church of England, but he wasn't happy with it. He believed that the Church had become corrupt and had strayed from true Christianity. People who believed as he did were called Puritans."

"Were they the ones who sailed in the Mayflower?" Carter asked.

"No," I replied. "Those were the Pilgrims."

"What was the difference?"

"The Pilgrims believed that the Church of England was too corrupt to be saved. They wanted to leave the Church of England altogether and worship in their own religion. And, they set up their colony in Plymouth, Massachusetts to do it.

"The Puritans believed that the Church of England *could* be changed - purified. They sailed to Boston right after the Pilgrims went to Plymouth and they set up a separate colony where they established the Church of England as the official religion, but with the changes they wanted."

"Couldn't they have done that in England, Gomps?" Hannah asked. "Why did they have to leave?"

"Because the Church of England persecuted them for criticizing it. They were kept from worshipping; they were arrested; they were attacked and even killed. The Church of England drove them out."

"I remember, now," she continued. "And, Anne's father, Francis, was a Puritan because he believed that the Church could be purified?"

"That's right, Hannah. And, Francis also believed in education for girls as well as boys."

"What was the big deal about that?" Carter asked.

"At that time, Carter, only boys were allowed to be educated."

"Why?"

"Two reasons, I think. One was the belief that only boys could learn."

"That was dumb," Carter said. "And...?"

"And, second, men wanted to keep power for themselves. I think that men in power understood the value of education. If women could be kept from learning, they couldn't become a threat to the men's power."

"Not too different from today," Hannah muttered.

"You think?" Mandy asked. "Oops, sorry, Gomps. I forgot your rule: no questions from the adults."

"That's OK," I said. "It's been a while since our last story times, but I'd like to keep that rule. Just the same, Hannah, do you really think men are trying to keep women from learning?"

"Not really," she replied, "but sometimes it seems that way. It's still true in some countries, though."

"You mean in the Middle East?"

"Yeah, and in Asia and Africa," she continued. "Haven't girls been hurt for trying to go to school?"

"Yes, they have, Hannah. A famous one is Malala Yousafzai of Pakistan. She was shot in the head and left for dead on her way to school."

"Yipes!" Carter exclaimed, "just for going to school?"

"Just for going," I said.

"How many have there been?" he continued.

"We don't know. That has been the practice in some countries for centuries, but until the last few years, it wasn't in the news."

"Why would they *do* that?" Hannah continued.

"To keep women subservient to men," I said.

"That's just wrong," Hannah concluded, "and stupid."

"And, barbaric," Carter added. "And, it's still done?"

"Yes, it still is," I said. "And, if you think about it, these men are cutting off some of the best ideas that their culture could have. They are excluding half the brainpower."

"Uh, I can't think about this anymore," Hannah declared. "What happened next?"

"To Anne?"

"Yeah."

"Well, Francis taught his sons at home," I continued, "as did just about all ministers, but he included Anne and her four sisters in the lessons, in defiance of the Church. While he got in trouble for doing this, he was able to give them all a good education.

"When she was 19, Anne's father died. A year later she married William Hutchinson, a London cloth merchant. Eventually, they had 14 children together."

"Fourteen?!" Hannah exclaimed. "That's a lotta kids!"

"Today it seems like a lot, but in those days, it wasn't unusual at all. What was unusual was that 12 of them lived beyond childhood."

"What do you mean?" Hannah asked.

"A lot of children died at an early age and lots of women died in childbirth. They didn't have the doctors and hospitals that we have today."

"Yipes!" she blurted.

"That's how it was," I said. "Now, during that time, Anne and William began to follow a minister by the name of John Cotton. He was a part of the Church of England, but he held Puritan beliefs. And, as Anne's father had, Cotton got in trouble with the Church.

"After hiding out to avoid punishment, Cotton fled to the New World in 1633, settling in the Massachusetts Bay Colony. There he found acceptance in the Puritan community.

"Hearing about Cotton's warm reception, Anne and William took their family and some friends and sailed to Massachusetts a year later. They settled in Boston and William set up shop as a cloth merchant, as he had in London.

"By this time, Anne had developed religious beliefs that were at odds with the Puritan way of thinking. And she got into a lot of trouble because of it."

"Why was that, Gomps?" asked Hannah.

"Well, first, she preached. In the beginning, she was a midwife — helping women with childbirth. In the process, she gave the new mothers religious guidance. It wasn't long before she started holding Bible meetings for women in her home, then full religious services. Hearing her message from their wives, the husbands began to attend, including, secretly, the Governor of the Bay Colony, Henry Vane."

"What was wrong with that?"

"The Puritans didn't allow women to lead worship services at that time."

"You're kidding!" Hannah exclaimed. "Didn't they come here for freedom of religion?"

"Well, the Puritans started acting like their religion was the preferred religion, just as the Church of England had," I said. "So anything that went against their beliefs was thought to be a threat to the Colony's leaders.

"But what she was preaching made things even worse. She preached beliefs opposite to some Puritan beliefs."

"Like what, Gomps?" Carter asked.

"It's kind of complicated, but, basically, she said that all you had to do to go to heaven was to have faith in God and in Jesus Christ and to ask them to forgive your sins. Puritan leaders believed that you could only get to heaven by following the laws of the Church."

"What laws?" Carter asked.

"Well, things like giving money, doing good works and obeying your minister," I said. "Anne believed that those kinds of laws were created by humans and not by God. If you truly believed that Jesus Christ was the Son of God and if you prayed to Him for forgiveness of your sins, you were good to go, as far as she was concerned."

"So she went up against the Church?" Carter continued.

"Yes, she did. And one other thing — she preached equal rights for women and Indians and against the Bay Colony government."

"The first Feminist!" Hannah shouted.

"I guess you could say that," I said, "probably the first in the New World, at least."

"No wonder she got in trouble," Carter said. "What happened to her?"

"Well, a trial was held in Boston. She stood up in court and repeated her beliefs. In the end, she was found guilty, excommunicated from the Church and banished from the Bay Colony."

"How did they banish her?" Carter asked.

"First, she was put under house arrest for four months. Then she was given three months to leave."

"How could they get away with that?" Carter asked.

"Well, by that time the leading ministers of the Puritan Church held a lot of sway over the Bay Colony government."

"But, Gomps, didn't you say that the Governor went to her services?" Carter continued.

"He did. He believed in religious tolerance and that led to his defeat. He was out after only one term."

"Wow," Carter said. "Sounds like the Puritan Church was just as bad as the Church of England."

"Sounds like it," I said, as I looked over to see Mandy and Mark smiling ever so slightly.

"Now," I continued, "while all this was going on, Anne had heard about what Roger Williams was doing in Rhode Island. He had set up a new colony that was open to people of any faith, including Baptists, Quakers and Jews.

"And Williams is probably the first to have called for a separation of Church and State. He termed it, '. . . a hedge or wall of Separation between the Garden of the Church and the Wilderness of the world.'"

"I thought Jefferson was the first to say that," Hannah said.

"He said it a little differently," I said. "His words were something like, '. . . a wall of separation between Church and State.'"

"Sounds like he stole it, though," Hannah said.

"Well, Williams's writings were pretty well known by the 1700s, so it would be hard to say that this was just a coincidence. Jefferson borrowed a lot of things he'd read. But enough of that. Let's get back to Anne's story.

"One of Anne's followers, John Clarke, approached Williams for help in relocating Anne's group to Rhode Island. Williams agreed and the group settled in what is now Portsmouth, Rhode Island. And, after a few years, Anne's husband, William, became an assistant to its Governor.

"There, Anne's thinking became more radical. She came to believe that people should govern themselves, free of any rules set by others. That meant no government and no Church structure.

"In 1641, Anne's husband, William, died, leaving Anne to manage their children and to preach by herself.

"Soon after William's death, the Massachusetts Bay Colony started trying to take over Portsmouth and the surrounding area. That would have been bad for Anne, so she made plans to move completely out of their reach.

"Anne knew families that had moved from Rhode Island to the Dutch settlement of New Netherlands, so she decided to follow them.

"A year later, Anne and her family moved to what is now the Bronx Borough of New York City. Unfortunately, this was an area that was soon to erupt into a war between the Dutch settlers and the local Indian tribe. Indians attacked Anne's house and killed her and everyone else, except one daughter who was off picking blueberries. The Indians took her hostage and exchanged her for ransom six years later.

"How come we never heard of her?" Hannah asked.

"Anne?"

"Yeah."

"Well, Anne's achievements have been debated ever since. But we now know that in addition to helping to settle Rhode Island, she stood up for what she believed in the face of her Church and colonial governments of men. She was likely the first woman to hold church services in the New World and the first to stand up to the male power structure of that time.

"You will find statues honoring her in Massachusetts and in Rhode Island as well as geographical features in her name. The Hutchinson River in New York was named for her, as was the Hutchinson River Parkway."

"Good," said Hannah.

"Yeah," said Carter. "I can see why she was pushed around, but that doesn't excuse it."

"I agree," I said. "But I think she doesn't get enough credit for her strength and courage, whatever her beliefs might have been. Under the circumstances, she was pretty super."

"Yeah," Hannah repeated, "super Anne Hutchinson."

"Well, that's it for this week," I said. "Next time I'm going to tell you about the Ginni Romettys of early America."

"Who's Ginni Rometty, Gomps?" Hannah asked.

"President of IBM Corporation."

"Never heard of her," Hannah remarked. "You, Carter?"

"Me either," he replied.

"You've probably never heard of any of these other women, either," I said, "but they all ran businesses."

"What?" Hannah blurted. "How could they do that? Women weren't allowed to do anything."

"You'll see," I said. "And, now you two get to your homework and I'll get home to Peach."

# 3

## AMAZONS OF BUSINESS

On the following Wednesday night, we gathered around after dinner for another story time.

"Last week I mentioned the name of Ginni Rometty," I said. "I'll bet you both looked her up, didn't you?"

"How did you know, Gomps?" Carter asked.

"Just a lucky guess. So, what did you find out?"

"First, you were wrong," he said. "She's not the President of IBM anymore; she's the Chairman of the Board and CEO."

"Oh, sorry," I said. "I stand corrected."

"She started as a computer engineer and worked her way up," he continued. "IBM was making computers and they started losing money at it. She thought they should stop making them and go into computer consulting and software. That's what they did and it worked. Now she's running the company."

"Very good, Carter," I said, "Hannah, how about you?"

"I found out she has won just about every business award you can get, for new ideas, profit increases, company growth, you name it. And she ran Watson, the IBM supercomputer that won the *Jeopardy* game show!"

"Great job, Hannah," I said. "You both got curious, didn't you?"

"Yeah," they chimed.

"So, why did I mention her when I could have chosen Oprah or Martha Stewart?" I asked.

"Like you said last week," Carter replied, "She's a successful woman that we never heard of."

"Right," I said, "and . . .?"

"You're going to tell us about successful businesswomen from colonial times that we never heard of," Hannah added.

"Exactly right, but, first, we have to take a look at what they were up against."

❧

"Women were expected to marry, and just about all of them did. And, as wives, they had children — a lot of them, in most cases. Along with raising and educating their children, they ran their households, but it wasn't like the housekeeping of today. They had no household equipment, so they had to do everything by hand, from cleaning, washing clothes, cooking, sewing and mending clothes, making butter and soap, to spinning cloth, and tending gardens and farm animals. Every colonial wife already had a full-time job, and it was hard."

"I'm glad I didn't live back then!" Hannah said.

"I know what you mean, Hannah," I said, "but that's what women did, so it was just accepted as a woman's way of life.

"When we talk about accomplished women, we have to remember that they had to run their households, too. And they were up against a system dominated by men.

"Men had been running things pretty much everywhere forever. Certainly in England the men ruled their families, the business world, the Kingdom, everything. Women were expected to run the home and raise the children.

"As the decades and centuries went by, this way of living became accepted. There were women, no doubt, who may not have been happy about it, but both sexes settled into that way of living.

"Is that about the way you figured it, Hannah?" I asked.

"Yeah," she replied, "women were kept in their place."

"'They were kept in their place' is a good way to put it," I continued, "but there was one big exception at the time and that was Queen Elizabeth I. She was born in 1533, the second child of King Henry VIII. She began at an early age to receive an education from a series of tutors. And by the time she became Queen at the age of 25, she was fluent in several languages, including Greek, Latin, French, Spanish, Flemish, and Italian.

"Elizabeth was the Queen of England for 44 years and during that time, she became a model of what an educated woman could do. More women began to get an education, thanks to what she had done."

"I didn't know that, Gomps," Hannah said. "I thought the rules were set in stone."

"Well, you could make a case for that," I said, "and plenty of people have, but it wasn't that cut-and-dried.

"Sadly, things didn't change as quickly in the colonies as they did in England. The old attitudes seemed to hang on longer here. If girls were to get an education, it was up to their fathers to OK it.

"Now, given that tradition, let's see how some women broke away from it.

℮↷

"So, here we go with businesswomen in the colonies — the Ginni Romettys of early America," I began.

"How many were there?" Carter asked.

"We don't have much of an idea."

"Why not?" he continued, "didn't they write letters and all?"

"You nailed it. Relatively few women wrote about their businesses or were written about. But we have enough to give us a good idea.

"Some women started businesses from scratch. They often began by doing things in their homes for their own families.

"Let's take clothing. A mother might have to start with raw wool sheared from the family sheep. She would card it . . ."

"What's 'card it'?" Carter interrupted.

"Hannah, can you answer that?" I asked.

"Isn't that when you brush the tangles out of the wool?" she replied.

"That's about right," I said. "If you've ever seen raw wool, it's all curly and tangled. Before you can do anything with it, you have to use a comb, called a card, to straighten out the fibers.

"After she carded the wool, she would spin it into yarn."

"Is that what a spinning wheel was for?" asked Carter.

"Yes, it was, Carter. She would sit at the wheel and feed the wool into it a little bit at a time. The spinning wheel would combine the wool fibers into yarn and wind it onto a spindle.

"When she had enough yarn, she would set up her loom, weave the yarn into cloth and sew clothing from it.

"Gomps, this is interesting and all, but what's it got to do with women in business?" Hannah asked.

"You asked the perfect question at the perfect time, Hannah. Let me answer with two questions: First, is this something you could do a few minutes at a time?"

"You mean spinning and weaving?" Carter replied.

"That's what I mean."

"No," he said. "It would take time to get set up, so you'd want to do a bunch of it at once."

"That's right," I said. "Now, the second question: would you want to guess in advance exactly how much cloth you would need?"

"No," Carter replied. "It would be too much of a pain to go back and start again if you ran out."

"Exactly," I said. "So, you'd make . . .?"

"Extra," said Hannah.

"That's right. And there you have the start of a business.

"A woman might have a lot of cloth left over. She might ask other women in the area if they would like to buy her leftovers. If she sold a lot, she might set up a little shop in a front room of her home. That would make it a 'cottage industry.'"

"I get it," Hannah said, "but if she were married, wouldn't her husband have control of it?"

"If he chose to, I guess, but if this little operation gave his wife extra money to buy things for the household, I think he'd just as soon let her run the whole thing, don't you? Don't forget, in those days the household operation was given over to the wives, anyway."

"I see what you mean, Gomps," Hannah acknowledged. "How often did this happen?"

"We don't know for sure. Maybe most women made extra of something and sold or traded it with their neighbors. Could have been cloth or candles or soap. Some of them set up shops in their homes to do it and some built their shops into businesses.

"Let's look at some examples. And, by the way, a good many of these women were Jewish."

"How come?" Carter asked.

"Well, it seems to have been part of Jewish traditions. Men made sure that traditions were followed and it took those who did it a lot of time."

"What kinds of traditions?" Hannah asked.

"Religious traditions, traditional laws, food handling, things like that.

"That left their wives to provide for their families, as well as keeping house and raising their children. Running businesses seemed like a logical way to do it.

"For example, Grace Levy was a Jewish widow with 12 children who set up a store in New York City in the 1730s. She sold a variety of things, like a general store. And, I will be telling you about other Jewish women as we go along.

"Abigail Adams, a Puritan and the wife of President John Adams, operated her own business in what they used to call 'notions' — ribbons and thread and buttons and such. Deborah Franklin, wife of Benjamin Franklin, opened a store in the front of their printing shop in Philadelphia. I'll tell you more about Abigail and Deborah on another night.

"Another businesswoman of the time was Mary Alexander," I continued. "She was born in 1693 and ran a fabric business in New York

City with her first husband, Samuel Prevoost. They had three children along the way, but he died around 1720 and Mary inherited the business."

"Women could inherit stuff?" Hannah asked.

"Yes, they could, Hannah, but let's make sure we know what it means to inherit something. What's inheritance?"

"Isn't that what you get when a relative dies?" Carter asked.

Mandy coughed and Mark quietly snickered.

"Well, that's a pretty direct way to say it," I said, "but that's it in a nutshell. Now, how do they know what they inherit?"

"With a 'will'?" Hannah said.

"That's right," I said. "Do you know what that is?"

"Isn't that when you write down what you give your relatives when you die?" Hannah replied.

"Right again," I said. "A will is a legal letter that you write before you die that tells your relatives which of your belongings, your 'estate,' you want each of them to get. And that would be their inheritance."

"Could women inherit stuff?" Carter asked.

"Yes, they could," I replied, "if the will said so."

"What if there was no will?" Hannah asked.

"You mean if a person didn't write a will before they died?" I said.

"Yeah."

"Then, a judge would decide. He was called the Judge of Probate and his court was called the Probate Court."

"Could he give inheritance to a woman?" Hannah asked.

"Yes, he could."

"But if women could inherit, what could they do with it?" Hannah continued.

"Great question, Hannah. That depended on whether or not they were married. Let's look at Mary Prevoost as an example.

"Mary inherited her husband Sam's business when he died, and soon after, she married James Alexander, a well-known lawyer and politician. Under the law, she could own her business, but James could decide what she could do with it."

"Huh?" Carter said.

"The law considered marriage as a legal partnership, Carter, under control of the husband. Anything the wife owned before the marriage, she would continue to own, but he had the say over it. She could also inherit while she was married, but he had the say over that, too.

"Mary continued to operate her company and we assume that she did so because James either said nothing or gave her the OK. As well he should have, since she made it one of the most successful businesses in New York. She also became a prominent member of New York society and an adviser to local politicians. She died in 1760, a wealthy woman.

"And Mary wasn't alone in running a business. Other women took in boarders to make extra money. Some turned their homes into boardinghouses. A few even bought other houses and turned them into hotels.

"Two who did were Hannah Moses of Philadelphia and Hetty Hayes of New York, both of them also Jewish. Hannah started and ran both a shop and a boardinghouse during the mid-1700s. Hetty built a boardinghouse business in New York City in the 1770s after the death of her husband."

"After," Hannah said.

"After," I said. "She didn't start until she was a widow."

"A woman could do that?" Hannah asked.

"Do what?" I asked.

"Start a business on her own," she replied.

"Absolutely," I said. "Things were very different for an unmarried woman. Women were considered under the law to be unmarried if they had never been married or if they were widowed and not remarried."

"A widow is a woman with a dead husband, right?" Carter interrupted.

Both Mark and Mandy looked up at the ceiling to keep from laughing.

"That's right, Carter," I replied.

"Just checking," he said.

"The law accepted that you had to give unmarried women the ability to provide for themselves," I continued.

"They kinda had to, didn't they," Carter said.

"How do you mean?" Hannah asked.

"Well, if they kept them from providing for themselves, they'd have to go on welfare," he concluded. "I don't think they wanted to do that."

"Did they have welfare, Gomps?" Hannah asked.

"Not the way we know it. Instead, a church, or relatives or neighbors would help them. Carter, you didn't mean welfare the way we have it today, did you?"

"Nah, I just meant it in general," he replied.

"Got it," Hannah said. "So, a widow or single woman would have to have some way to support her family, if she could."

"That's how it worked," I said.

"Back to the law. Unmarried women, like Hetty, could use anything they inherited, and they could buy and sell property just like a man. And, if a married woman became widowed, any property that was hers before she married was still hers, plus any property she inherited from her husband."

"Hmmm," Hannah hummed. "Might make you think twice about marrying or remarrying."

"Well, I wouldn't go that far," I said. "The New World was still a place that wasn't easy to prosper in, even for a man, but I'm sure there were women who thought that, including the ones I'm going to tell you about next week - the 'business magnates'."

"What's a 'magnate,' Gomps?" Carter asked.

"You're going to have to wait until next week for that, Carter."

# 4

## AMAZON MAGNATES

After dinner, I started our story time.

"Last week, I promised to tell you about business magnates who were women. First, what's a 'magnate'?"

"You're not talking about an iron bar that sticks to things, are you," Carter quipped.

"No."

"You're talking about someone who's a big deal?"

"Hannah?" I asked. "What do you think?"

"Someone who owns big businesses."

"You're both right," I said. "Magnates are people who have big businesses and earn a lot of money from them. One of them was Esther Pinheiro.

"In 1710, Isaac Pinheiro died, leaving his entire business to his wife Esther. He had an import-export business, and she took over the whole thing — his merchant ship, the *Neptune*, and his offices in New York, Boston, Amsterdam, and the Caribbean island of Nevis.

"Esther ran the company until at least 1718 trading sugar, molasses, flour, lumber, and fish. She often sailed aboard the *Neptune* to watch over her goods and to cut deals when she arrived in port. And Esther earned a lot of money.

"Another businesswoman was Abigail Minis of Savannah, Georgia, who inherited her husband's operations in 1757. She took over his mercantile company, his plantation, and a successful tavern. Through the years, she added over one thousand acres to the plantation. She died in 1794 at the age of 93, no doubt a wealthy woman.

"Speaking of plantations, we can't overlook a woman who not only ran plantations, but was quite a botanist, too. Her name was Eliza Pinckney. She was born in 1722 on the Caribbean island of Antigua to George Lucas, a lieutenant colonel in the British Army, and his wife, Ann.

"Eliza was the oldest of four children, having one sister and two brothers. When their children reached the age of nine, the Lucases sent them to boarding school in London."

"The girls, too?" Carter asked.

"Yes, Carter, the girls, too. George was one of those fathers who believed that his daughters should be educated.

"Eliza wrote back to her father that her favorite subject was botany and that her education was more important to her than any fortune he could have given her.

"Eliza returned from boarding school to Antigua just as her father inherited three rice plantations in South Carolina. Sensing danger to the family from the growing tension between England and Spain, the Lucases moved to one of the plantations in 1738. Eliza was 16 years old.

"Shortly after, Col. Lucas was recalled to Antigua, and he left Eliza in charge of one of the plantations. It had 600 acres, 20 slaves, and a thriving rice farm. In addition. . ."

"Wait, Gomps," Hannah interrupted. "What do you mean 'in charge'?"

"She ran the place."

"You mean like a president?" she continued.

"Yes, she called the shots."

"At 16?"

"At 16," I replied. "And if you have a hard time with that, you're going to have a harder time with this: her father made her the supervisor of the men who ran his other two plantations. She was responsible for a total of 5,000 acres."

"Holy cow!" Carter exclaimed.

"That's amazing, Gomps," Hannah concluded, "but what about her mother? Wouldn't she have been the one to do it?"

"We don't know for sure. Her mother was reported to be sickly or an invalid and to have died while Eliza was still young. Or, maybe Colonel Lucas wanted his wife to concentrate on raising the children, or maybe he thought Eliza could run the operation better. It seems he had some ideas that he thought were best suited for Eliza to carry out."

"What ideas, Gomps?" Carter asked.

"There were parts of his plantations that weren't good for growing rice. Col. Lucas wanted to make them productive by growing other crops there. So, from Antigua he sent Eliza seeds of all kinds — cotton, ginger, and alfalfa among them. Eliza experimented with all of them and kept detailed records.

"None of the crops proved promising until he sent her indigo seeds."

"What's indigo?" Carter asked.

"You know," Hannah said. "It's the plant that they made blue dye from. Gomps told us about it last year."

"Oh, yeah," Carter said, "I remember now."

"Right," I continued. "Indigo became a really important crop. Before that, clothes were drab homespun. Suddenly, blue colors became all the rage.

"So, after three years of experimenting, Eliza came up with a way to grow and process indigo profitably. She shared her methods with neighboring farmers, and before long indigo production in South Carolina increased more than twenty-five times over. By the start of the Revolutionary War, indigo was more than one-third of the colony's economy."

"Wow!" said Carter. "She was a big deal."

"Yes, Carter, she was," I said, "but there's still more to her story.

"In 1744, the wife of Charles Pinckney, a farmer on a neighboring plantation, died, childless. Charles was a big deal himself. In addition to his plantation, he was an attorney and politician who was active in the colonial government.

"Eliza and Charles knew one another, since they had neighboring plantations. They courted and married that same year, just as Eliza was publishing the results of her experiments with indigo. She was just 22.

"Eliza and Charles had four children, three of whom survived. She wrote in her journal, 'I am resolved to be a good mother to my children, to pray for them, to set them good examples, (and) to give them good advice . . .'

"Sadly, 14 years after they were married, Charles came down with malaria and died. Eliza inherited his plantations and his other property and became the manager of it all. She operated the plantations at a profit and became a fierce and generous supporter of the independence movement.

"In the years that followed, Eliza's children made names for themselves as well. Her son Charles was a signer of the Constitution and ran for both Vice President and President. Son, Thomas, became the Ambassador to Great Britain, and as an extraordinary envoy to Spain, he negotiated major treaties with them, one of which bore his name. He also ran for Vice President.

"Eliza lived another 35 years. She got sick and went to Philadelphia for treatment and died there at the age of 71. She was so well regarded that one of the pallbearers at her funeral was George Washington. And, in 1989, she was the first woman named to the South Carolina Business Hall of Fame."

"Amazing, Gomps," said Hannah. "Do you think the other planters tried to keep her from running her plantations?"

"You mean because she was a woman?"

"Yeah."

"Not after she showed them how to double their profits," I said.

"Hah," Carter chortled. "Guess not."

"She was one in a million," Hannah concluded.

"Not at all," I said.

"What do you mean, Gomps?" Hannah asked.

"I haven't told you about Caty Greene yet and her story is even more amazing. But it will have to wait until next time. I'm tired and you two have things to do."

# 5

# FROM BLOCK ISLAND TO CUMBERLAND ISLAND

"Last time, I said that I would tell you about Caty Greene," I started in as soon as dinner was over. "She turns out to have been quite the character.

"Caty Greene was born to John and Phebe Littlefield in 1755 on Block Island, Rhode Island, the third child of five and the first daughter. She was given the nicknames of Caty and Kitty from the beginning. We'll call her Caty.

"When Caty was just 10 years old, her mother died and her father sent her to a relative on the Rhode Island mainland to be educated.

"We don't know how they met, exactly, but when she was 19, Caty married Nathanael Greene. Nathanael was tutored by family friend Ezra Stiles, the future President of Yale University, but had no formal education.

"Nathanael's father died soon after the marriage, and Nathanael took over the operation of the family's foundry business. You can visit their house in Coventry, Rhode Island. It has been restored and furnished as it was originally. The foundry was right nearby."

"What's a foundry, Gomps?" Carter asked.

"It's a kind of factory, Carter, where they make things from metal. In those days, the factories were rather small and they cast things from molten iron or beat them into shape from iron bars."

"Like a blacksmith?"

"Like a blacksmith, but bigger."

"Got it."

"That same year," I continued, "Nathanael set up a local militia and started as a private. He had a pronounced limp, so instead of serving in the infantry, he concentrated on military tactics. A year later, he joined the Continental Army. That left the management of the family and property to Caty, as with so many other military wives.

"Within a year, Nathanael was promoted to brigadier general and was assigned to the command of the troops in Boston."

"Whoa, wait a minute, Gomps," Carter interrupted, "From private to general in one year?"

"That's right," I said. "Sounds impossible, doesn't it, especially with the limp? But I guess it shows what a natural leader he was and how much he had learned about military tactics.

"George Washington apparently saw great ability in Nathanael from his command in Boston. Washington transferred him to Brooklyn, New York and assigned him to the command of the preparations for the Battle of Brooklyn. But Nathanael got sick before the actual battle and had to go back to Rhode Island to get well.

"After he was back to health, Greene was promoted to Major General and given command of a division in the Battle of Monmouth . . ."

"Wasn't that the battle where Molly Pitcher fired the cannon?" Hannah asked.

"Yes, it was, Hannah. Good memory."

"Did Nathanael know her?" she continued.

"I don't know," I said. "I don't recall reading any reference to it, at least. Why don't you do a little research and see what you can find out?"

"Good idea," she said. "I'll give it a try."

"Back to the Greene's," I said. "A year later, Nathanael was made the commanding general for the whole southern Continental Army, and he put together the strategy that drove General Cornwallis and the British Army to Yorktown, Virginia and final surrender. The war was won."

"Gomps, that's interesting and all, but what about Caty?" Hannah asked. "Isn't this story about her?"

"You read my mind. I had to go over what Nathanael did so you can understand what Caty did."

"OK," Hannah said, "but can you tell that part now?"

"I was just about to," I said.

"In case you hadn't noticed," Carter interrupted, "I was interested in what *Nathanael* did."

"Well, good for you," Hannah said.

"Hey, you two," I said, "knock it off or I'll stop here."

"Sorry, Gomps," Hannah said. "It sounded like Carter was trying to get brownie points."

"I wasn't," he said. "I like hearing about the battles."

"Can I go on now?" I asked.

"Yeah." "Yeah," they both conceded.

"Good," I said. "I told you about the places that Nathanael had been because Caty often went with him. Remember that George Washington's wife, Martha, had set up camps for the soldiers' wives?"

"Yeah," Carter said, "isn't that where Molly Pitcher went?"

"That's right, Carter.

"Caty Greene followed Nathanael to those camps just as Molly had followed her husband. There was one important complication for Caty, though. Can you guess what it was?"

"Nathanael was an officer, so their camp was better?" Hannah suggested.

"Good try," I said, "but the wives of officers and enlisted men stayed in the same camps. Carter?"

"Was she sick?" he guessed.

"No," I replied. "The answer is, she sometimes took her children with her."

"To the camps?" Hannah asked.

"Yup."

"How long would they stay?" Carter asked.

"As long as the troops were set up there. Would have been days and weeks, and in the cases of Morristown and Valley Forge, the whole winter."

"How old were the kids?" Hannah asked.

"I don't know their exact ages, Hannah. Three of them were born during these years."

"Yipes," Hannah said, "that must have been hard. Did she have to go?"

"You mean go to the camps?" I asked.

"Yeah."

"No, she could have stayed home."

"You said 'sometimes,'" Carter said. "The children didn't always go with her?"

"Apparently not."

"Why did she take them?" he continued.

"I haven't found any evidence of her thoughts on that, so we have to guess. Maybe she missed them when she went alone. Maybe Nathanael wanted to see them. Maybe she couldn't make arrangements for them to stay at home."

"Didn't she have relatives or slaves who could take care of them?" Hannah asked.

"Hannah, you've been doing some studying about this, haven't you," I said.

"Yeah," she said, "lots of people in New England had slaves that worked in the house and helped take care of the kids."

"All the evidence shows that she left the children with family or friends when she didn't take them along," I said. "I haven't found any mention of slaves."

"She must have been tough to have been able to do all that," Hannah concluded.

"Yes, I think so, too," I said. "But that's just the beginning.

"While in command of the southern army, Nathanael saw the poor state of his troops' uniforms. Their clothing was mismatched, patched together and in tatters. Some didn't have boots and had to wrap their feet with rags or go barefoot.

"When Congress hesitated to approve money for new uniforms, Nathanael personally guaranteed to uniform dealers the cost of replacing them."

"Wow," said Carter. "So he was paying out of his own pocket?"

"In effect, he was, Carter. His guarantee was that the suppliers would be paid by Congress at the end of the war and he would back it up out of his own money, in case they didn't. He decided that he would worry about settling up after the war.

"Unfortunately, the uniform dealers took advantage of Nathanael and ran up enormous bills in his name. At the end of the war, Congress didn't pay and he was presented with debts he couldn't afford, and he went broke.

"In an effort to pay off what he owed, Nathanael went to the South Carolina and Georgia legislatures and asked for grants of land as payment for his service. They agreed and gave him Boone's Barony, a plantation in South Carolina, and Dungeness and Mulberry Grove - two plantations in Georgia.

"He immediately sold Boone's Barony to pay off part of his debt, and he and Caty decided to live at Mulberry Grove. So, in 1785, Caty picked up lock, stock and barrel from Rhode Island and moved the family to Georgia, along with their children's tutor, Phineas Miller, a Yale University graduate. They knew no one in Georgia and had to start their lives over from scratch.

"Nathanael and Caty were determined to pay off the rest of his debt, and they worked hard to earn the money. The main crops at Mulberry Grove were cotton and rice. Nathanael and Caty had to learn quickly the business of running a plantation.

"Sadly, less than a year later, Nathanael overworked himself in the fields and was hit with sunstroke. He died on June 19, 1786, leaving Caty with a family to raise, two plantations to run, and bills to pay.

"Caty went right to work. She promoted Phineas Miller from tutor to plantation manager and together they made Mulberry Grove profitable.

"Six years later, Caty applied to the U.S. Congress for money to pay off the rest of her debt. Congress recognized Nathanael's patriotism and passed a law to approve it. President George Washington signed it as soon as it reached his desk. Caty was finally out of debt."

"Phew," said Hannah, "She never gave up, did she, Gomps?"

"No, Hannah, she never did. She admitted that the debt was hers to pay and she paid it.

"In the same year, a strange series of events unfolded. Caty met a young man who was tutoring the children on a neighboring farm. His name was Eli Whitney."

"I've heard that name before," Hannah interrupted.

"Me too," said Carter. "Didn't he invent something?"

"Yes, he did and that's the strange part of the story. Whitney was from Massachusetts and graduated from Yale University, but his interest was in mechanical things and not in the liberal arts. So, while he took jobs as a tutor, he kept tinkering with machinery. One of those tutoring jobs was in Georgia, near Mulberry Grove.

"It so happened that Phineas Miller, being a Yale graduate himself, had known Whitney there. So when Whitney showed up (or maybe Miller invited him over), there was a natural connection.

"It wasn't long before Whitney and Caty began talking about the cotton business and the processing of raw cotton. Caty showed him how cotton seed had to be removed from cotton by hand, and Whitney became interested in making a machine to do it.

"Here's where there is disagreement among the historians about who did what. Some say that Caty did the first design; others say it was Whitney. In either case, Whitney built a machine that used metal fingers to separate the seeds from the cotton — and it worked. They called it the cotton gin."

"Why was it called a 'gin', Gomps?" Carter asked. "Was he drinking in his machine shop?"

"Good question," I chortled. "I wondered that, too. Whitney called it a 'cotton engine' and that got shortened to 'gin.'"

"Simple enough," he said.

"In an act of generosity," I continued, "Caty and Eli decided to make a few of the 'gins' and give them to their neighbors. They worked so well that Eli was encouraged to build a factory to make and sell them. Caty invested in the plan and Whitney returned to Connecticut to set up shop.

"Unfortunately, there were no patent laws at the time, and the Georgia neighbors got the same idea. Whitney's cotton gin sold well until his price was undercut by their competition, and Caty lost her investment in the resulting price war.

"Whitney stayed in Connecticut to invent something else and Caty stayed at Mulberry Grove."

"Why didn't she go back to Rhode Island?" Hannah asked. "Isn't that where her family was?"

"You'd think so, Hannah, except she had fallen in love with her plantation manager, Phineas Miller."

"Ohhhhh," said Hannah. "No wonder."

"After she lost her money, she and Miller continued to run the plantation together, and in 1796 they married.

"But Caty's financial losses forced her to sell Mulberry Grove and two years later, they moved into her one remaining property – Dungeness, on Cumberland Island on the Georgia coast. There they continued to farm until Phineas's death five years later. Caty remained at Dungeness, doing her best to get along, until she died in 1814. And, that's the story of Caty Littlefield Greene."

"Wow," Hannah said, "what a life! She was tough to do all those things and still keep her family together."

"Yeah," observed Carter, "she supported the troops, ran plantations, and, maybe, designed the cotton gin. I like her."

"So do I," I said.

# 6

# THE FIRST WOMEN ATTORNEYS

"How did all these married women do so many things on their own, if the law said that their husbands were in charge?" Hannah asked as we sat down for the next week's story.

"Good question, Hannah, and I'm not sure I can answer it fully. I figure that in some cases the husbands were busy with other things and were happy to have their wives carry the ball. In others, I think the wives just went ahead without permission and dared their husbands to stop them. Don't forget the wives were bringing in good money."

"That would do it for me," added Carter.

"But, there had to be women who *were* kept from doing things by their husbands," Hannah persisted.

"I suppose," I said, "but do you think that *all* wives wanted the extra burden?"

"I guess not," she continued. "You'd have to be super-determined to want to raise a family and run a business."

"But they could if they wanted to," I said.

"Yeah," she admitted, "they could."

"OK," I said. "Let's go back to New England, where Sarah Kemble Knight made a name for herself. She was born in Boston to a merchant family, but we don't know much else about her childhood. In 1688, she married Captain Richard Knight, a shipmaster who was much older than she. He died a few years later. We don't know if she inherited his shipping business, but we do know that she started many other enterprises herself.

"Sarah started a writing school in 1705, during which time she taught herself the law so that she could work as a court 'scrivener,' someone who copied legal documents. While not a trained lawyer, she built up a business settling estates and other routine legal matters – what we would call a legal assistant today. At the same time, she set up a store in the front of her home and opened a boarding house elsewhere in Boston.

"Along the way, Sarah bought land in the New York/Connecticut area and, after traveling there to provide legal assistance to a relative, moved permanently in order to oversee her holdings. She died in 1727, leaving an estate of 1,800 pounds to her surviving relatives."

"Gomps, how do you know all this?" Carter asked.

"She kept a diary. Wrote it all down, and you can see it on the Internet."

"Her own handwriting?" he asked.

"Yup. It's hard to make out in places, but it will give you an idea of how people spoke at the time."

"Cool," he said.

"Gomps, you said that Sarah Knight taught herself the law, like a legal assistant," Hannah said. "Were there any women lawyers?"

"Yes, there were. The first was Margaret Brent. She was a 37-year-old, unmarried Englishwoman who came to the Maryland Colony with her brothers and sisters in 1638. She got a 70-acre land grant from the governor, Lord Calvert, and started a boardinghouse with her sister, Mary. She added more land to her holdings and, in the process, became friendly with Calvert.

"In an effort to defend the colony against invasion, Calvert had hired soldiers from Virginia, but he didn't pay them. They were furious and protested, but Calvert died before the soldiers could get their money.

"Before he died, Calvert had named Margaret the administrator of his will. She sold off part of his estate and paid the soldiers, and that calmed them down.

"Later, the Maryland Colonial Court named Margaret as the attorney for Calvert's brother, Lord Baltimore, who had stayed in England. As Baltimore's lawyer, she was to represent him in matters that couldn't wait for letters to go back and forth to England.

"In 1648, Margaret appeared before the colonial Assembly to present Lord Calvert's estate and to explain her decisions in administering it, especially in paying the soldiers. She appeared in court at other times to represent both Calvert and Lord Baltimore. The last time, she presented the interests of Lord Baltimore in a civil case against a Thomas Cornwallis.

"In appreciation of Margaret's skill, the colonial Assembly wrote a letter of commendation to Lord Baltimore, saying, 'it (the estate) was better for the Colony's safety at that time in her hands than in any man's ... for the soldiers would never have treated any others with that civility and respect.'"

"So, it was because she was a woman," Hannah said, "not because she was good."

"Well, let me ask you a question," I said. "If she hadn't been good, how would the Assembly have worded that letter? Do you think they would have overlooked her work if they were ready to jump on any evidence to prove that a woman couldn't do it?"

"I guess not," she replied.

"To me, the letter was just the opposite," I said. "They admitted that, maybe, there are some things where a woman can do the job better. In this case, she thought of a way — paying the men by selling off part of the estate. And, coming from someone for whom they had been taught respect, it worked. That letter was recognition for a job well done. See what I mean?"

"Yeah," she said. "I hadn't thought of it that way."

"OK, now let's pick up where we left off," I said.

"Another woman lawyer was Susanna Wright, a rural Pennsylvania poet and healer. In 1745, she began writing wills, deeds and other legal documents for her neighbors. Before long, she was settling land disputes and giving legal advice.

"Lucy Terry Prince of Vermont, a former slave, was still another. She argued before the U.S. Supreme Court in a land dispute in 1797."

"The Supreme Court? A slave?" Carter said.

"A former slave," I said. "She was born in Africa, captured as an infant, made a slave in the United States, and bought into freedom by her husband, Abijah Prince."

"What was the case about?" he continued.

"She and Abijah owned a farm in Vermont and their neighbor tried to claim some of their land as his. The case went all the way to the Supreme Court."

"Didn't they have a lawyer, Gomps?" Hannah asked.

"Yes, it appears that they had two, but she argued the case herself anyway. She must have been pretty strong-willed to have brushed them aside."

"And smart," Hannah added.

"She won the case," I continued, "and Justice Samuel Chase praised her argument as 'better than any Vermont lawyer.'"

"Won the case," Carter said.

"Yes, she won it," I said, "and, as far as we know, she is the first woman and the first African American to argue a case before the Supreme Court, let alone win."

"But what about Elizabeth Key?" Hannah asked. "Wasn't she before this?"

"You mean the slave from Virginia?" I said.

"Yeah," Hannah continued. "She was African."

"And a slave," I said, "but she argued before the Virginia Assembly, not the Supreme Court."

"Oh, yeah," Hannah said, "but she won her case, didn't she."

"Yes, she did," I said, "and they made her a free woman.

"So, those are the woman attorneys that we know of.

"Do you think there were more?" Hannah asked.

"Probably, but if so, they were more like Sarah Knight – doing legal work without appearing in court. I haven't come across any other reports of women's names in court proceedings. But I haven't searched specifically for that."

"So, if there were women lawyers," Hannah continued, "were there any woman doctors?"

"It depends," I replied. "If you mean medical doctors, physicians, I haven't come across any. It took medical school training in England to be a doctor, and that appears to have been limited to men. But if you mean women in the healing arts, they were everywhere."

"Weren't there any medical schools in the colonies?" Carter asked.

"Not yet, there weren't, not ones that could give a medical degree."

"What were the women?" he continued.

"Midwives," I replied.

"What are those?"

"Women who help other women with childbirth.

"For example, Bridget Fuller delivered three babies during the crossing of the Mayflower and continued as a midwife in Plymouth for 44 years. Anne Hutchinson was a midwife in addition to being a preacher."

"You mean the Anne Hutchinson who got kicked out of Massachusetts?" Carter asked.

"Yes, that Anne Hutchinson," I replied.

"Wow, she was busy," he said. "Who else?"

"Pick a town and you'd find them. Ruth Barnaby, Elizabeth Phillips and Ann Eliot were among hundreds of midwives who helped women with childbirth. Many of them had established practices, just like the doctors of today. In fact, because of their knowledge of medicine, they were often asked to treat diseases and injuries as a doctor would."

"They were *actual* doctors," Hannah declared.

"In practice, maybe, yes, but not with a medical degree. It appears that the first woman to get a medical degree – and become a formal doctor - was Elizabeth Blackwell in 1849."

"Did midwives make house calls?" she asked.

"Oh, yes, just like doctors. The home was the only place where they could deliver babies or treat the sick. The first hospital in America wasn't founded until 1751."

"Couldn't have been very sanitary, in people's houses," she said. "It must have been easy for the mother to get an infection."

"No doubt," I said. "I'm sure that was a big reason why so many women died from childbirth. Same for diseases and injuries.

"And, that's it for tonight's story. Next time, we'll look at women in the publishing business."

And with that I bid them all a good night.

# 7

# PUBLISHING – A POPULAR BUSINESS

"What is it about the printing and newspaper business that would have attracted the women of the time?" I began this session.

"What do you mean, Gomps?" Hannah replied.

"A lot of Colonial women seem to have gotten into that profession," I said. "Most continued newspaper businesses started by their deceased husbands, but not all.

"One was Anne Catherine Green, a mother of 14 children. She took over the family print shop and the *Maryland Gazette* in 1767 when her husband died. Another woman by the name of Margaret Draper took over the *Massachusetts Gazette* in 1774. Still another, Hannah Watson, became the publisher of the *Connecticut Courant*, now the *Hartford Courant*, when her husband died in 1777.

"But not all takeovers were from dead husbands. Ann Franklin, Benjamin Franklin's sister-in-law, took over the *Newport Mercury* upon the death of her son in 1762.

"Mary Goddard took over the publication of *The Maryland Journal* from her brother, William. He had been in business with Benjamin Franklin in the national post office system that Franklin had created. When William left Maryland in 1774 to promote the postal system, Mary kept the *Journal* going.

"Mary became so successful and well known that she was named the Postmaster of Baltimore and published the first copy of the Declaration of Independence with the names of the signers included. Along the way, she also ran William's book printing business and started a bookstore of her own.

"William returned from the postal service ten years later and, after bitter arguments, forced Mary out of the business. Not to be denied, she continued as Baltimore's Postmaster for five more years and ran her bookshop, expanding it to include stationery and groceries, until her death in 1816."

"That's odd," said Carter. "Why do you think so many women were in the newspaper business?"

"Well, I'll tell you what I think," I said, "and you can tell me what you think."

"OK," they chimed.

"I think that women saw what England was doing to the Colonies and many had strong opinions about it. Women were not included in official colonial government, but they still wanted their opinions to be heard. By running a newspaper, women could publish their opinions as editorials and control the news stories they printed. Some of them became very influential that way."

"Gomps, you said that women were not included in colonial government," Hannah said. "That sounds like a nice way of saying they were kept out by the men."

"I suppose you're right," I said, "but if that's the only part of the story you concentrate on, you're going to miss a lot of women's accomplishments."

"Yeah," Hannah said. "I suppose so, but it just makes me mad."

"Understood, but there were men who supported women's rights, too. Another time, I'll tell you about more of them, but one was James Warren, the husband of a famous poet and playwright, Mercy Otis Warren. He wrote to John Adams that it was 'at his particular desire' that Mercy had written her play, *the Ghost*, which advocated for women's rights. And, don't forget the number of husbands and fathers who made possible the education of their wives and daughters. John Adams was one."

"There weren't that many, though, were there?" she said.

"Maybe not. Carter, what do you think?"

"I think that's just how it was," he replied. "When did Women's Liberation start?"

"The most recent movement started maybe 40 or 50 years ago."

"Takes time," he said. "Who's next?"

Everyone smirked at Carter's desire to get back to the story, except Hannah. But she said nothing.

"There's one more newspaperwoman I want to tell you about, and she was probably the most important one of all. She not only ran her dead husband's paper, but started two on her own. This is the story of Mary Crouch.

"Mary Crouch was born Mary Wilkinson, one of four children, in Smithfield, Rhode Island in 1740. She married Charles Crouch in 1763 in Providence and they had one child – a girl.

"Charles had been born in 1735 in Charleston, South Carolina."

"South Carolina?" Hannah interrupted. "How did he get to Rhode Island?"

"On a horse?" I joked. "But, seriously, that's a great question. All I could find out was that he had been a printer's apprentice as a teen in South Carolina and had gone to Rhode Island to be a printer."

"Do we know why?" Hannah asked.

"It appears that he had strong opinions about the colonies gaining independence from England and his boss in South Carolina was against it. They argued, but that's all I know. Why don't you see if you can find out more?"

"In my spare time," she replied. "But, yeah, I'll put it on my list. What about you, Carter? Why don't you look it up?"

"Right," he said, "after I finish my paper on Black Holes."

"All right, Carter," I said, "we don't need a snide remark, but you made your point. Hannah, looks like this one's up to you.

"Now, back to the Crouch family. It seems that Charles's Providence printing business didn't go so well. He and Mary moved to Charleston, South Carolina, in 1764, just a year after they were married.

"Charles set up a print shop there right away and, within a year, started a newspaper he called the *South Carolina Gazette and Country Journal.*"

"How did that one do?" Carter asked.

"Pretty well, Carter. There had been two other newspapers in Charleston, but both were put out of business by the Stamp Act. So Charles had no competition."

"What was the Stamp Act, again, Gomps?" Carter asked. "I remember your telling us last year, but I don't remember what it had to do with newspapers."

"Glad you asked. The Stamp Act was a law passed by the English Parliament that taxed everything in the Colonies that was printed. The King collected on every colonial deed, loan, check, will, letter, calendar, diploma, gambling bet, license, advertisement, and newspaper. The law required that every document had to be stamped by the tax collector to show that the tax had been paid."

"Oh, I remember now," Carter said. "And the tax must have made the newspapers too expensive, and the publishers went broke."

"That's right," I said.

"So wouldn't the Stamp Act have done the same to Charles's newspaper?"

"You would think so, but Charles was smart. He set up operations in a house rather than a shop, so it was harder for the tax collector to track him down. A year later, Parliament repealed the Stamp Act, but by that time the others were out of business.

"So the *Gazette and Journal* became the only newspaper in Charleston. And Charles voiced his opinions through it in support of colonial independence. As did his wife Mary."

"How did she do that?" Hannah asked.

"Through anonymous letters to the editor and essays. The paper was very successful, and Mary helped out when deadlines were tight. But about seven years later Charles died, and Mary took over the business."

"As a widow, she could do it," Hannah concluded.

"That's right," I said. "Sad as Charles's death was, Mary was free to own and operate the paper and the print shop.

"If anything, Mary's views favoring independence were even stronger than Charles's had been, and she used the newspaper to further them.

"Do you remember the Boston Tea Party?" I asked.

"When the colonists threw a shipload of tea into the harbor to protest the taxes?" Carter asked.

"Yes, Carter."

"What's that got to do with a newspaper in Charleston?" Hannah asked.

"A lot," I replied. "After the colonists had thrown the tea in Boston harbor, the English closed the port of Boston and blockaded it. Word of the British action spread like wildfire, reaching Charleston in a matter of days.

"Mary became incensed over the treatment of Boston and worried that the British might do the same to Charleston. She wrote letters to the editor under made-up names . . ."

"Letters to her own paper?" Carter asked.

"That's right, Carter. She used letters to voice her opinion in addition to the editorials that she wrote.

"Then Mary decided that Boston needed help from South Carolina. She started a campaign in her paper to boycott the purchase of tea in the southern colonies. She donated her own money to Boston and, in editorials, asked others to contribute. She printed the names of the people who had given money – more than 100 of them - and even bought rice and sent it to Boston for free.

"Weren't the English mad at her?" Hannah asked. "They must have known."

"They knew, and they were angry. She took a big risk in doing what she did, but that's how strongly she felt. She also lost friends who had become supporters of England. And she received threats on the newspaper and on her life."

"Yipes," exclaimed Carter. "What did she do?"

"At some point, Mary stopped publishing the *Gazette and Journal*," I said, "and in 1778 she started a second newspaper – the *Charleston Gazette* - under her own name.

"This new newspaper was even more out-spoken than *The Gazette and Journal.* Mary published letters to the editor which openly called for revolution. One of them was from Catharine Macaulay, the English historian who supported independence."

"Didn't Mary get in trouble with the British again?" Carter asked.

"Worse than that. Two years after she printed her first issue, British troops occupied Charleston. Charlestonians who were loyal to the King told the troops where she was and that put her in danger. She had to shut down the paper and get out of town."

"Where'd she go, Gomps?"

"Back to New England - to Salem, Massachusetts. As soon as she arrived, she started another newspaper — the *Salem Gazette* — again under her own name. Sadly, that paper published only 36 issues before she had to close it down — this time for lack of advertising. It just didn't make a profit.

"In 1781, Mary moved back to Providence, where she lived the rest of her days in peace."

"Wow, she did a lot more than just print a newspaper, Gomps," Hannah concluded. "She really was part of the Founding!"

"You know, I agree with you," I said. "By her support of Boston and her open support for independence, she showed the colonies that people in the South were patriots, too."

"What about you, Carter?" I asked. "What did you get from Mary's story?"

"She didn't give up," he said. "She could have closed up the first paper and moved back to Rhode Island when her husband died, but she was brave and toughed it out. I guess that's kinda like the Pilgrims, huh?"

"Yeah," I replied, "you've got a point there."

"What about you, Gomps?" he continued. "Why did you tell us this story?"

"Mary was another example of women who did more than what was expected of them. In her case, what she did had ripple effects throughout the Revolutionary War and through our new nation. That's a pretty important legacy."

"OK, you two," Mark said. "It's time for Gomps to go home and time for you to do your homework. And when you're done with that, find something extra and do that."

"Funny, Dad," Carter said.

# 8

# THE MYSTERY OF THE SPIES

"Hey, guys," I said, "look who's here!" I had just walked in the door at the kids' house with their grandmother, Peach.

"Peach!" they shouted.

"Hi, kids," she replied, as they ran up and gave her a hug.

"Hi, Mom," said Mandy.

"Hi, Peach," said Mark. "What brings you here?"

"Gomps!" she said.

Everyone groaned.

"Funny," said Mark. "No, really."

"Peach has been doing research on colonial times for the mystery novel she's writing," I said. "She knows more about tonight's subject than I do. So I thought she'd tell the story better."

"You're going to tell us a mystery story, Peach?" asked Carter.

"Something like that," she said.

"About what?" asked Hannah.

"Oh, that's a mystery," Peach replied with a twinkle in her eye, and everyone laughed. "Dinner first. Mandy, what can I do to help?"

℘

"Tonight we're going to stay in the Revolutionary War period," I started out. "More women than just Molly Pitcher and Margaret Corbin were involved. And Peach is going to tell us about some of them.

"Peach, you know the ground rules, don't you?" I asked.

"I think so," she replied. "The kids can ask questions any time they want, and Mandy and Mark have to keep quiet."

"Right," said Hannah. "So, what's the mystery?"

"Spies, tonight and masqueraders, next time," said Peach.

"Oooo," said Hannah. "Women were spies?"

"Sure were."

"What are masqueraders?" Carter asked.

"That's the biggest mystery of all," Peach replied. "Masqueraders are people who pretend to be someone else, like when you dress up for Halloween."

"Oh, yeah," he said.

"Let's start with the spies," Peach began. "Many Colonial women were just as patriotic as the men, and spying gave them the perfect chance to help the cause for independence.

"Most men didn't think women were smart enough to understand their talk of war, so when they talked about strategy, they thought nothing of it if women overheard them. And that gave women an advantage, because plenty of them understood very well.

"British troops occupied most cities, and colonial women moved among the soldiers as waitresses, maids, and ordinary townspeople. They kept their eyes and ears open to what the British were doing and planning, and some of them passed along what they learned to the Continental Army.

"They set up secret ways to report what was going on, and . . ."

"You mean like code and secret messages?" Carter blurted.

"Just like that," Peach answered.

"Cool," he said.

"Let me tell you about some of these women," Peach continued.

"Gomps said he told you about one of them last year. Remember the wife of the British General who spilled the beans?"

"Was that the one who told Paul Revere that the British were coming?" Carter offered.

"That's the one – Margaret Kemble Gage," Peach replied. "She grew up in the New Jersey colony, not in England, and she had secret sympathy for independence. She was married to General Gage, who was the British commander in Boston. And she was a friend of Joseph Warren, a doctor who shared her sympathies and who knew Paul Revere.

"People always wondered how Paul Revere found out when the British troops would start their march to Lexington and Concord.

Looks like Margaret overheard her husband making plans – he may have even told her - and she told Dr. Warren about them. Dr. Warren told Paul Revere and that set the warning in motion."

"What happened to her?" Hannah asked. "Did the General find out?"

"There was no proof," Peach replied. "In fact, some people think it may not have been Margaret at all. Still, the General sent her to England three months later with their children. Maybe he wanted her out of harm's way or maybe he suspected her as the source of the warning and just wanted her out of the way, period.

"Either way, after his defeats, General Gage was relieved of command by the King and brought back to England four months after he sent Margaret. They never left England again."

"What do you think, Peach?" asked Carter. "Was it Margaret?"

"Yes, it was," she replied. "If someone else spilled the beans, we would have found out by now."

"Do you think General Gage knew?" Carter continued.

"He knew," she replied again with certainty.

"For sure?" Carter asked.

"He wouldn't have remembered telling her?" she continued, "and it just so happens that the rebels are waiting for them in Concord? He may not have been a good general, but he was no dummy."

"Why didn't he do something about it?" he persisted.

"He loved her," she said. "That's the only explanation. They lived together in England, in the same house, until he died twelve years later. By the way, she lived another 37 years after that and never remarried."

"So he forgave her?" Hannah asked.

"Yes," said Peach.

"How can you be so sure?" Carter asked.

"I wasn't a psychotherapist for 30 years for nothing," she replied. "After a while, you get an intuition for these things."

She paused, then continued: "Now, Margaret Gage wasn't the only woman who spied. Let me tell you about some others.

"Lydia Barrington was raised in Dublin, Ireland. At 24, she married William Darragh, a tutor, and they moved to Philadelphia in 1755. William got a job as a tutor there and Lydia became a midwife.

"When the British Army occupied Philadelphia in 1777, they moved their troops right into people's homes."

"They could do that?" Hannah asked.

"Yes," Peach replied. "Didn't Gomps tell you about the Quartering Act?"

"Oh, yeah," Hannah said, "I remember now."

"I thought so," Peach continued. "Well, the British moved their troops right into the Darragh's house. Thinking that Lydia couldn't understand war strategy, the officers spoke together openly while she hung around. One version of the story even has her hiding in a closet to listen in.

"One night, the British officers planned a sneak attack on an American camp at White Marsh, Maryland. Lydia heard them and wrote a note to George Washington warning him of the plan.

"The next morning, Lydia got permission from the British officers to cross the battle lines to buy flour. Instead, she went to a tavern where she knew American troops hung out. She found a man named Elias Boudinot there and handed him the note. Boudinot was a friend of Washington and the head of the nearby prison. Boudinot delivered Lydia's note while she scurried back, picking up the flour along the way.

"Two days later, the British attacked, but the Americans were waiting for them and drove them back. Smelling a rat, they asked Lydia if she knew of anyone in the house who might have heard them, never imagining that a woman might have been able to do that. She, of course, denied everything and was never found out."

"So how do we know?" Carter asked.

"Boudinot's diary," Peach replied. "He made detailed notes and you can see them online."

"Aha," Carter said.

"That was a good story, Peach," Hannah concluded. "Were there other women spies?"

"Quite a few," Peach replied, "but we're not sure how many. And some spied for the British."

"For the British?" Hannah exclaimed.

"Yes, there were women who spied for the British," Peach replied, "including one famous one."

"How can that be?" Hannah continued.

"Didn't Gomps tell you about British sympathizers – the Loyalists?" Peach asked.

"Um, yeah," she replied, "but I didn't think they would go that far."

"Well, a few did," Peach said.

"One was known as Miss Jenny. She was a French woman living in the colonies and spying for the British. She was caught in New York while trying to get back to the British side. First the French, then George Washington himself tried to get her to confess, but she never did. They even cut off all her hair to shame her into talking.

"Miss Jenny was finally let go and she made it across to the British side. There, she made her report, got her reward and left. She was never heard from again."

"Peach, if the Americans couldn't get her to confess, how do we know she was a spy?" Hannah asked.

"A German army officer, Baron Ottendorf, who worked for the British, wrote it down in a letter to General Clinton," Peach replied. "That's online, too.

"Another who spied was Ann Bates, an American schoolteacher and Loyalist, who worked for General Clinton himself. She pretended to be a peddler and sold goods to the American troops while she counted the soldiers and their weapons.

"The Americans fell victim to the same kind of thinking about women that the British had and, as Ann moved among them, she over-heard their plans. She even got into George Washington's camp several times and reported key information back to the British.

"Did she do that alone?" Carter asked.

"That's a great question, Carter," said Peach. "She didn't. She was part of a spy ring that was run by a man that I think you know – Major Andre."

"Don't remember that name," Hannah said.

"Me, either," Carter said.

"If I said that he was the contact for Benedict Arnold, would that jog your memories?" Peach continued.

"Oh, yeah," they both chirped.

"Well, along with Ann Bates," Peach continued, "Benedict Arnold was the center of probably the most damaging women's spy story of the War – his wife!"

"Really?" Hannah said.

"Yessir," Peach replied. "Benedict Arnold's wife was a British spy."

"Tell us; tell us," they begged.

"You think I wouldn't?" Peach chided. "This is the story of Peggy Shippen Arnold.

"Peggy was born in 1760 to a wealthy family of Loyalists in Philadelphia. After the British occupied Philadelphia, her family entertained British officers in their home. It was at one of these parties that Peggy met Major John Andre and the two struck up a friendship.

"After the British left Philadelphia, the Continentals put Benedict Arnold in charge of running the city, and that's when Peggy met *him*.

"From the beginning, Arnold complained to Peggy about how the Americans were mistreating him. Being a Loyalist, Peggy lent a sympathetic ear and introduced him to Major Andre. A series of secret letters passed between Andre and Arnold with Peggy as the go-between. She even wrote some of them in code and invisible ink."

"No way!" Hannah exclaimed. "Really?"

"Really. Is that hard to believe?"

"Sorta."

"Why? Is the story far-fetched or is it because you can't imagine a woman doing that?"

"Both, I think."

"Well," said Peach, "men and women are equal, aren't they?" Then, she paused.

Finally, Hannah said, "Well, I guess a woman could do that."

"There's good and bad wherever you go," Peach pronounced. "The best we can do is to keep a lookout for the bad. Now, back to Peggy, because her story isn't over.

"Peggy and Benedict got married in Philadelphia in 1779, during the time when his corruption in running the city came to light. She defended him and helped him get the charges reduced. Still and all, his resentment toward the American side grew, and he kept up his communications with Major Andre through Peggy.

"Benedict was fired from his job in Philadelphia, and he was so resentful that he decided to turn traitor and go over to the British side in return for a military commission. Through Peggy and Andre, he planned to get command of the West Point Military Academy so he could weaken it for British invasion. When he got the appointment to the Academy, Peggy joined him there.

"As we know, the plot was foiled when the Americans captured Major Andre on his way to the British lines with the plans in hand. Word of the capture got back to Benedict at the Academy and he escaped and headed for the British lines himself, leaving Peggy behind."

"What a rat!" Hannah announced.

"Don't be so sure," Peach replied. "We think that she offered to stay behind."

"Why would she do that?" Hannah continued.

"To stall the Americans and keep them from catching up with him," Peach said.

"The American officers suspected that Peggy must have known something, and they questioned her. She went into a hysterical fit, screaming and thrashing around for hours. That gave Benedict time to get through."

"Didn't they see through that?" Carter asked.

"Apparently not," Peach replied. "Her act was so good that even George Washington couldn't believe that she was pretending, and they stopped questioning her.

"As soon as the coast was clear, she made her way back to Philadelphia, but the authorities still suspected what she had done, so her father took her to New York City. There she got together with Benedict again and they sailed for London, unscathed.

"She spent the rest of her days in London, dying of cancer in 1804."

"And all this is true?" asked Carter.

"Oh, yes," Peach replied, "every bit of it is documented in original letters, messages, and reports."

"Whew," Hannah sighed. "That is some story."

"Sure is," said Carter. "Thanks."

"I'm not done," Peach pronounced.

"There's more?" Mandy asked.

"Yes," replied Peach, "more mysteries, if we have time."

"I'm afraid not, Mom," Mandy said. "These kids have things to do. You'll have to finish next time."

"It's OK by me," Peach said. "Kids? What do you think?"

"We'd like to hear more," Hannah said, "but it will be better if we have another session for it."

"Yeah, we would get you twice in a row," Carter said, "no offense, Gomps."

"None taken," I said. And Peach and I said our goodbyes and left.

# 9

# THE MYSTERY OF THE MASQUERADERS

"Tonight's mystery is about the masqueraders," Peach began. "Let me start by asking you a question: suppose a woman was so patriotic that she wanted to fight on the front lines. How would she do it?"

"No way!" blurted Hannah. "Women fought as soldiers?"

"Really?" said Carter. "Not just in back like Molly Pitcher?"

"That's right, at the front, with a musket," Peach replied. "How would she do it?"

"But, but, they wouldn't let her!" Hannah said.

"She would know that they wouldn't let her," Peach continued. "So how would she do it?"

"You mean just one day?" Hannah asked.

"Nope, marching, fighting, camping, day after day," Peach persisted. "How would she do it?"

Peach waited to let the idea sink in and give them a chance to think of a way. As she waited, she glanced over at Mandy and Mark. Both had bemused smiles on their faces.

Finally, Carter said, "You said masquerader before. Did she dress as a man?"

"Hannah, what do you think?" Peach asked.

"But there would have been men all around her," she replied. "How would she change clothes, go to the bathroom, hide her . . . you know?"

"Congratulations, kids," Peach exclaimed. "You've solved the mystery. Let's see how she did it.

⌾

"The most famous masquerader was Deborah Sampson, a young woman of Massachusetts. We don't know much about her except that she was determined to fight alongside the men.

"Deborah sewed a uniform and bound herself up with yards of linen, if you know what I mean, and enlisted in the infantry under the name Robert Shirtliffe."

"Couldn't they tell?" Carter asked.

"Apparently she was tall and strong," Peach replied, "and I'm sure that she spoke in as low a voice as she could. And it looks like the Continental Army needed volunteers so much that they didn't ask too many questions.

"All told, Deborah served three years, fighting on the front lines . . ."

"Three *years*?" Hannah shouted. "No way she could have gotten away with it for that long. No way."

"Maybe she didn't *get away with it*," Peach replied. "The legend says that the men had a nickname for her – 'Molly.'"

"Molly?" Hannah said, "They knew?"

"There're two possibilities," Peach answered. "Either they thought Robert was gay or they knew Robert was a woman and accepted her. Carter, what do you think?"

"It's possible they thought it was a gay man," he replied, "but that wouldn't have been the end of it. Did they do anything to Robert?"

"You mean like harassment?"

"Yeah."

"Not that anyone reported," Peach replied.

"Then it means that she fought well enough and they just accepted her," he concluded.

"Hannah, you buy that?" Peach asked.

"Makes sense, but I still can't believe it," she replied. "Three years? And she was in battle?"

"In battle and wounded . . . twice. The first time, she was cut in the head by a sword in hand-to-hand combat."

"Hand-to-hand?" Carter exclaimed. "She fought that close?"

"Sure did. The second time she was hit in the leg by a musket ball. To keep her secret she treated herself instead of going to the field hospital.

"Deborah recovered pretty well from both injuries, although her leg didn't heal right, but she got sick from a disease that was sweeping the ranks - dysentery.

"She was sent behind the lines to recover and the doctor who treated her discovered her secret."

"So the jig was up," Hannah declared.

"Not at all," said Peach. "He said nothing and moved her to his home for long-term recovery. There he wrote a letter to George Washington, and when she was well enough, she delivered it herself.

"She must have been scared to death," said Hannah.

"I imagine," said Peach, "but it seems Washington didn't say anything either, and, instead, wrote a letter discharging her from the Army with his thanks."

"What happened to her?" Hannah asked.

"She got married, had a family and one day got a letter from Washington, who was by this time the President. The letter asked her to come to Philadelphia to receive a military pension and a grant of land with the thanks of Congress.

"Now, I know what you're going to ask," Peach continued. "Is all of this true?"

"Yeah," Carter said.

"You're right to be skeptical," Peach replied, "and there are descriptions that differ on the details, but there's no denying that Deborah served for three years, on the front lines, dressed in Army uniform.

And it's on the record that Washington wrote her discharge and that Congress gave her the pension and land."

"Wow, she was brave," said Hannah.

"I'll say," said Carter. "It's hard to believe, but sounds like it's true."

"Were there others?" Hannah asked.

"Others, what?" Peach replied.

"At the beginning, you said masqueraders," Hannah continued, "more than one."

"Oh, yes," Peach said. "We don't know how many masqueraded as Deborah did, but there are quite a few others that we know at least something about. Let's start with the Martin sisters.

"Grace and Rachel Martin of South Carolina stayed home while their husbands, who were brothers, fought with the Continental Army. In 1780 the sisters heard that a British messenger would be riding their way with an important letter. They dressed as men, grabbed their guns, stopped the messenger on the road, and took the letter from him. Then, they sent the letter to the Continental lines and it helped the Army to avoid an ambush. And, their disguises had been so good that the messenger stopped at their house for lodging afterward and he never recognized them."

"Amazing," Hannah said.

"Several other women dressed in uniform and fought," Peach continued. "There was Anna Marie Lane of Virginia, Elizabeth Gilmore of Pennsylvania, Sally St. Clair of South Carolina, who was killed in the Battle of Savannah, and 'Mad Ann' Bailey, who dressed as an Indian scout and fought Indians.

"We also have documentary evidence of women in Capt. James Green's New Jersey Regiment. Of the 114 soldiers listed in the Regiment, 19 were women – some wives, some spinsters and some widows. All are listed in the same way as the men.

"So that's the mystery of the masqueraders. There were plenty of women who disguised themselves as men and fought right alongside them."

"I'm a believer," said a smiling Mark.

"Me, too," said Carter.

"Women really did a lot, didn't they," concluded Hannah.

"Yes, they did, sweetheart," said Peach. "But, there's one more woman I want to tell you about. Her name was Nancy Hart and she was a spy and fighter all rolled into one.

"Nancy was born Nancy Ann Morgan in 1735 in North Carolina. Does the name Morgan ring a bell?"

"No," replied Carter, "but from the sound of your voice it sounds like it should."

"Hannah?" Peach asked, "any idea?"

"Nope, me neither," she replied. "But I think Carter's right – she's going to turn out to be someone."

"I'll spare you the suspense," Peach said. "Her uncle was General Dan Morgan, one of the most important generals in the southern

Continental Army. On top of that, she was the first cousin of Daniel Boone!"

"I remember now," Carter exclaimed. "That was some family."

"Sure was," added Hannah. "What did *she* do?"

"Nancy grew up on a farm and became a big, strong woman and headstrong, too," Peach said. "She married Benjamin Hart, a South Carolina farmer, in 1755, and they had a daughter.

"Both Nancy and Benjamin were fierce supporters of independence, but their farm was in an area filled with Loyalists and British army camps. It was also in Cherokee Indian territory. The Cherokees called her 'War Woman.'"

"Because she fought them so hard?" Hannah asked.

"I think so," Peach replied. "Anyway, Nancy decided to take full advantage of their location in British territory. On several occasions, she dressed as a man and wandered through British camps pretending to be mentally retarded. The British soldiers saw no threat in this person and continued to talk about their war plans freely. Every time Nancy heard something useful, she wandered away and crossed enemy lines to deliver the news to the Continentals, sometimes miles away.

"One day when Benjamin was in the fields, six British soldiers showed up at their door. They were hungry and demanded that Nancy feed them. When she refused they went out back, shot Nancy's only turkey and handed it to her at gunpoint.

"Whoa," said Hannah, "hard to argue with that."

"Maybe," Peach replied, "but apparently Nancy formed a plan at that instant and put it into action. She agreed to fix the turkey for them, and while it was cooking, she chatted with them and offered them liquor. The more she talked the more they drank until they were drunk. As she expected, they all fell asleep.

"At that point, she took one of their muskets and handed it to her daughter, telling her to take it outside, away from the house. She took a second one and did the same, handing it to her daughter.

"When she took the third musket, though, all hell broke loose. One of the soldiers woke up and rushed Nancy to get the gun away from her. He never made it — Nancy shot him."

"Oh!" Hannah exclaimed.

"Of course, that woke up the others," Peach continued, "and another soldier started after her. At the same time, Nancy took back the second musket from her daughter. The second soldier never made it, either. She shot him, too.

"Nancy grabbed the third musket and held the other four soldiers at gunpoint. By this time, Benjamin got back to the house on the run. He grabbed another musket and helped Nancy keep them at bay.

"Nancy and Benjamin talked about what to do with the remaining four soldiers. He wanted to deliver them to the nearest Continental Army camp where they would be put in a prison camp. Nancy would have none of that — she wanted to hang them."

"Hang them? *She* wanted to do it?" Carter exclaimed.

"Apparently," Peach said.

"Who won the argument?" Hannah asked.

"I'll let you be the judge," Peach replied. "Decades later, archeologists dug up the Hart farm to see if they could find evidence of the story. There, in a common grave they found six human skeletons. What do you think?"

"I believe it," gulped Hannah.

"No doubt there," declared Carter.

"What happened to her?" Hannah asked.

"That's the last we know of Nancy," Peach replied. "There's no other record of her doing anything in the War. We're not even sure when she died."

"That was quite a story, Peach," said Mandy, "but now it's time for these two to get to their homework. Thanks for a great night. It's no wonder you're such a great writer."

"Uh, oh," I said, "I hope I don't lose my job."

"Don't worry, Gomps," said Hannah. "We love your stories just as much."

"All right, you two," said Mark. "Off you go to your books."

"Ooookaaay," said Carter. "Will you be here next time, Peach?"

"No," said Peach. "This won't be a regular thing for me, but I might be back if I have another good one to tell."

"We hope so," said Hannah.

# 10

## MIDNIGHT RIDERS

"'Listen my children and you shall hear,'" I began on the next Wednesday, 'of the midnight ride of Paul Revere.' Do you remember that story from last year?"

"Wasn't that when Paul Revere rode at night to warn the towns that the British were coming?" Hannah offered.

"That's right," I said. "And do you remember those words?"

"'Listen my children,' you mean?" she asked.

"Yes," I said.

"That was a poem, wasn't it?"

"Yes, it was," I replied. "The poem was called 'Paul Revere's Ride' and it was written by Longfellow.

"Now, what if I told you that there were other midnight riders like that?"

"There were?" Carter said.

"Yup, and what if I told you that the riders were women?"

"Really?" he said.

"Really."

"At one time, together?"

"No, at different times - at least three of them."

"Amazing," he said.

"Hannah, you buy that?" I asked.

"Of course," she said, "but how did they do it?"

"Let me tell you about them.  I'll start with Sybil Ludington.

"Sybil was born in 1761 in Kent, New York, to Henry and Abigail Ludington. She was the oldest of twelve children. Sybil's dad operated a gristmill and was a colonel in the local militia.

"In April 1777, the British landed a force of 2,000 soldiers on the Connecticut coast, and they marched to Danbury to destroy weapons and supplies that the Continental Army had stored in a warehouse.

"A Continental dispatcher rode from Danbury to the Ludington home, arriving at nine o'clock that night. He warned Colonel Ludington of the British attack and asked him to gather his militia and rush to Danbury to defend the warehouse.

"Sybil overheard the dispatcher and decided to take matters into her own hands. She was just 16 years old.

"She saddled her horse and set out at once. During the night, she rode over 40 miles, through five towns, knocking on doors and telling the militiamen where to gather. She got back home at dawn, exhausted, but successful.

"Colonel Ludington led the militia to Danbury as fast as possible, but they were too late to save the warehouse. Nonetheless, they found the British force, fought them in the Battle of Ridgefield, and drove them back to their ships."

"What happened to Sybil?" Hannah asked.

"That was the only war action that she was in, that we know about, but she was given a commendation by George Washington, and the records show her application for a military pension. We don't know if she got it.

"After the war, Sybil married Edward Ogden, who was a lawyer, an innkeeper, and a farmer. They had one child and lived together in the Catskill Mountains area. She died in 1839 at the age of 77."

"Neat," Carter observed. "She was brave. By the way, how far did Paul Revere ride?"

"About 20 miles."

"So she rode twice as far," he concluded.

"Yup."

"And at night, like him," he continued.

"Yup."

"Cool."

"Who's next?" Hannah asked.

"How about Deborah Champion? She was the 22 year old daughter of Henry Champion, the General of Supply for the Continental Army. The family was living in the New London, Connecticut area, and in

1775 General Champion needed to get secret letters through enemy lines to George Washington, who was in Boston.

"Deborah insisted that she could do it. Posing as an old woman, she hid the letters in her clothing and rode for two days. Despite being stopped by the British several times, she got through and delivered the letters to Washington's camp.

"Emily Geiger of South Carolina was another messenger. She was 18 when she overheard a Continental officer tell her father of General Greene's need to get reinforcements from General Sumter, who was camped 70 miles away. With their united forces, General Greene and General Sumter would attack the advancing British General – Lord Rawdon.

"Emily volunteered to deliver the message. Her father wrote it down, and off she went. After several close calls, her luck ran out and she was stopped by British lookouts. They brought her back to their camp and called for a woman to search her. While waiting for the woman to arrive, Emily memorized the note, tore it up and ate it!"

"Ate it!" Hannah exclaimed. "Ha, ha. What a cool trick!"

"That was quick thinking, that's for sure," I said.

"The woman searched Emily and found nothing, so the British let her go. She rode the rest of the way to General Sumter's camp, recited the note she'd memorized, and rode back home.

"General Sumter marched his troops to General Greene's camp, and together they defeated Lord Rawdon in the Battle of Eutaw Springs. That victory helped turn the tide of the southern campaign in our favor.

"Behethland Moore would be another midnight rider, if you count canoes," I continued.

"Canoes?" Carter blurted. "What do you mean, canoes?"

"Would you count canoes as equal to horses?" I asked. "Behethland was the 15-year-old daughter of a Continental Army Captain in the Laurens District of South Carolina. One night, her father learned of a British force that was advancing toward another Continental regiment upriver.

"Behethland volunteered to warn them. Under cover of night, she paddled her canoe up the river to the Continental camp. She arrived in time and the regiment there was saved."

"In that case, canoes should count," Hannah announced.

"I think so, too," said Carter.

"How about swimming?" I asked.

"Swimming?" Hannah replied.

"Yeah, swimming. Should swimming count as midnight riding?"

"C'mon, Gomps, let's hear it," Carter cracked. "We know you got another one there."

"OK, ya got me. This one's about Dicey Langston.

"Dicey was another South Carolina girl who delivered messages about British plans."

"South Carolina, again?" Hannah blurted. "Independence wasn't just in the north."

"That's for sure — here's Dicey's story.

"She was born to a small family of patriots in a region of South Carolina Loyalists. By the time she was 15, her brothers had joined a patriot militia regiment that was camped at Little Eden, some miles away.

"As Dicey played with her friends at their Loyalist homes, she often overheard their parents talk about British plans to invade certain areas.

"One day, Dicey heard that the British were marching to Little Eden. She rushed home and set out on foot to warn her brothers. On her route, she had to cross the Tyger River. With no way to do it other than swimming, she plunged in, clothes and all, and swam to the other side. From there, she ran soaking wet to her brothers in time for them to clear out. The British found nothing when they arrived."

"Whew," said Hannah. "It sounds like there were a bunch of women, girls, even, who delivered messages. Is that true, Gomps?"

"Yes, it appears to be. Patriotism wasn't restricted to men, and this was something that women could do if they had the strength and determination. There were more than the ones I've mentioned, I'm sure. But that's all we have time for tonight, so I'll let myself out while you get ready for bed. G'night, all."

"G'night, Gomps," they chimed together.

# 11

## SUPER SLAVE WOMEN

"Tonight, I want to go back to a subject we covered in some detail last year – slavery," I began this Wednesday, "slavery of black Africans.

"This time, though, I want to tell you about black African women slaves who made their mark in colonial America."

"You mean like Elizabeth Key?" Hannah asked.

"Yes," I said.

"You mentioned her before, but I'd like to hear the story again," Hannah said.

"Me, too," Carter said.

"OK, here goes," I said.

❧

"Elizabeth Key's story got my attention because it seemed like she ignored what she wasn't supposed to be able to do and just went ahead and did it. I'm always impressed with that kind of attitude.

"Elizabeth Key was the daughter of an African slave woman and a white English man in Virginia. Her father was likely the owner of her mother, and whether they had a romantic relationship or he just took advantage of her, we know that they were not married."

"In any event, the year was 1656 and Elizabeth had been declared by her father to be of 'negro' race and, therefore, a slave. Once she grew up, though, she didn't think she should be a slave just because she was half Negro. Her father was white and free, after all. She figured that she was just as much free as not. So she decided to fight it."

"And she fought it with a lawsuit," Carter said.

"That's right, Carter," I said. "She took her father to court."

"That's still surprising," said Hannah. "I can't believe that the court would let a slave do that."

"Well, it was only 50 years since the first Virginia settlement," I said. "The courts had just been set up. They were still using English Common Law, and I think it was the first case of this kind that they had. They probably figured that a black slave woman wouldn't be able to argue in court, anyway."

"They found out that they were wrong, didn't they," declared Hannah.

"Yes, they did," I concurred. "She stood right up and argued her case. And, as you know, she . . ."

"Won!" said Carter.

"And the court made her a free woman!" Hannah added.

"Yes," I said, "but we know that the Virginia colony couldn't allow that decision to apply to other slaves.

"The slave owners figured that if they didn't do something, other slaves would find out about it and file lawsuits, too. So, six years later, the Virginia House of Burgesses passed a law that any child of a slave was also a slave, and that was the end of that."

"You gotta figure that's what they'd do," Hannah said. "They had too much money invested. Who's next?"

"Phillis Wheatley," I replied.

"Never heard of her," Hannah said.

"Me, either," Carter added.

"Phillis Wheatley was an African girl who was sold into slavery from her West African home at seven years old," I began. "She was sent to Boston on board the slave ship *Phillis*. There, she was bought by the Wheatley family of Boston.

"John Wheatley was a wealthy storekeeper and tailor and with his wife, Susannah, had a son and a daughter. As was the custom at the time, they named Phillis after the ship that brought her to America and gave her their last name. She was made a household slave from the beginning.

"The Wheatley's soon noticed that Phillis was really smart, and they included Phillis in the tutoring of their children. Within five years, Phillis was reading Greek and Latin. She especially took to poetry, reading Thomas Gray, Milton, and Alexander Pope, as well as the classics.

"Amazing," Hannah declared.

"One day," I continued, "another household slave saw Phillis copying words from a book in the family library. Upon being told, rather than forbidding it, the Wheatley's encouraged Phillis to write.

"Phillis became most famous for her poetry. She wrote her first poem at thirteen – 'On the Death of the Rev'd. George Whitefield.' I brought a copy along to read to you.

'HAIL, happy saint! on thine immortal throne,

Possest of glory, life, and bliss unknown;

We hear no more the music of thy tongue;

Thy wonted auditories cease to throng.

Thy sermons in unequalled accents flowed,

And ev'ry bosom with devotion glowed;

Thou didst, in strains of eloquence refined,

Inflame the heart, and captivate the mind.

Unhappy, we the setting sun deplore,

So glorious once, but ah! it shines no more.'

I paused as we all sat in stunned silence.

"In case you're wondering, that was only the first of five stanzas," I said.

"And she wrote that at 13?" Hannah marveled.

"Yes."

"Do you have any more of her stuff with you?" Carter asked.

"How did I know you would ask?" I replied, as I took out other pages.

"This one is a poem she wrote about her enslavement. By this time, she had become a Christian. It's called 'On Being Brought From Africa To America.'

'T WAS mercy brought me from my pagan land,

Taught my benighted soul to understand

That there's a God--that there's a Saviour too:

Once I redemption neither sought nor knew.

Some view our sable race with scornful eye--

'Their color is a diabolic dye.'

Remember, Christians, Negroes black as Cain

May be refined, and join the angelic train.'

"And, finally, here's her tribute to George Washington, entitled 'His Excellency George Washington.' After four stanzas, it ends:

'Proceed, great chief, with virtue on thy side,

Thy ev'ry action let the Goddess guide.

A crown, a mansion, and a throne that shine,

With gold unfading, WASHINGTON! Be thine.'

"Amazing," Hannah observed.

"Yes, it is," I concurred. "She wrote at least three books of poetry. They were published in both America and England. The English publications earned her a trip to London when she was twenty. She returned later that year after having met the Lord Mayor of London, among other officials.

"Phillis was freed in 1775 through the will of John Wheatley, upon his death. She married John Peters, a free black man who was a grocer. They fell on hard times and he was sent to debtors' prison in 1784. She died later that year, at 31, probably in childbirth."

"What a story, Gomps," Hannah exclaimed. "Her poetry was beautiful. Can we read more of it?"

"You sure can. One of her books is titled *Memoir and Poems of Phillis Wheatley*. It was published in 1834 and entered into the Massachusetts archives that same year by an Act of Congress. It's online."

"Amazing what you can get online these days, isn't it," said Carter. "Any more slave stories?"

"There are probably many more, but I'll share just one more, since it's getting late.

"This last one may be the most famous. Her name was Elizabeth Freeman, but she was known as 'Mum Bett'.

"Records of Mum Bett's early life are sketchy. It appears that she was born into slavery in 1742 or so on the farm of Pieter Hogeboom in eastern New York. When Hogeboom's daughter, Hannah, married John Ashley of Sheffield, Massachusetts, Pieter gave Mum Bett to them as a wedding present.

"John Ashley was a Yale lawyer and wealthy landowner. He was also active in western Massachusetts politics. In fact, his house was probably the place where the Sheffield Resolves were signed."

"What's that, the Sheffield Resolves?" Hannah asked.

"Good question. I don't think I've mentioned it before. The Sheffield Resolves was a statement of human rights that the Sheffield townspeople put into the form of a petition in 1773. They did it to object to England's taxes and unfair treatment of the colonies. Some say it was like an early Declaration of Independence."

"How so?" she asked.

"Well, here's the First Resolve and you can decide for yourself: 'Mankind in a state of nature are equal, free, and independent of each other, and have a right to the undisturbed enjoyment of their lives, their liberty and property,'"

"Whoa, see what you mean," Hannah said. "It sounds like Jefferson had read this before he wrote the Declaration."

"It sure does," I said. "He borrowed from a lot of writings for the Declaration. He didn't just dream it up. But let's get back to our story.

"Now, Mum Bett could neither read nor write, but she understood spoken English very well. Shortly after the passage of the Massachusetts Constitution, it was to be read to the townspeople from the meeting house steps. Mum Bett went to hear it and was struck by the words declaring that all men are created equal.

"Shortly after, she went to Theodore Sedgwick, a local attorney who was active in the anti-slavery movement. She told him that she thought that, since she lived in Massachusetts, the Constitution applied to her as well as anyone else and that she should be free as a result.

"Sedgwick agreed and took up her case. They added Brom, another of the Ashley family's slaves, to the case and sought the assistance of Tapping Reeve, the founder of the Litchfield Law School, one of the first and most influential law schools in America.

"Together, they sued in the Great Barrington County Court in the case called Brom and Bett v. Ashley, and, in 1781, a jury set Mum Bett and Brom free. This case became the precedent that ended slavery in Massachusetts."

"What happened to her, Gomps?" Carter asked.

"The Ashleys asked her to work for them for wages, but she turned them down. Hannah Ashley was no friend of Mum Bett, having once burned her with a hot shovel when Mum Bett tried to defend a younger slave whom Hannah was trying to hit.

"Instead, Mum Bett bought her own house in Stockbridge and worked for the Sedgwicks. A Sedgwick daughter, Catharine, wrote Mum Bett's history years later, and you can read it online.

"Mum Bett lived to her mid-eighties and is buried in the Sedgwick family plot in Stockbridge. She is widely thought of as a clear-thinking and brave pioneer in the antislavery story."

"I can see that," Hannah observed. "There must have been a lot of slaves who thought of themselves as equal, just as much as their . . . I hate to call them owners, especially after they heard the Declaration of Independence. But she stood up for herself. That took a lot of guts."

"Yeah," concurred Carter, "Her and Elizabeth Key. I wonder if Mum Bett ever heard of Elizabeth."

"I searched their records, but there's no evidence that she did," I replied. "I think she was moved by the words that she heard on those meeting house steps and by her own self-regard. Something clicked and she decided to risk it. Good thing she did, don't you think?"

"Yeah!" both kids chimed.

# 12

## ROSIE THE RIVETER

"Who's heard of Rosie the Riveter?" I started off the next week.

"I've heard the name," Hannah replied, "but that's about it. Was it in World War II?"

"Carter? How about you? Ever heard of her?" I asked.

"Nope, doesn't ring a bell," he replied.

"Rosie the Riveter was a fictitious character from the Second World War," I said. "She symbolized the women who made guns and other war materiel while the men were away fighting.

"All kinds of weapons, equipment, and supplies were needed for the troops, but there were too few men to work in the factories. So they hired women to do it."

"Were there enough who could?" Carter asked.

"They weren't sure at first, Carter, but they discovered that with training there were plenty of women who could do the work just as well as men."

"I coulda told you that," Hannah pronounced.

"Sure, Hannah, but did you know that there were some women who already had worked at riveting by this time?"

"You mean, literally?" she replied.

"Literally," I said. "Some colonial women were in the smithing trade – had metal workshops. We don't know much beyond their names, but one was Mary Knight of Virginia who was a blacksmith and had a forge in 1715. Another was a Mrs. Paris of Philadelphia who worked in brass. We know about her because in 1730 she put a want ad for an apprentice in the paper when her first one ran away. There was Mary Stoddard, who was a blacksmith in Litchfield, Connecticut, in the 1770's, after taking over her dead husband's business. And, in 1774 there was a shoe smith in Chester, Pennsylvania named Elizabeth Humphreys."

"And they worked with hammers and anvils?" Hannah asked.

"Yes, they did - each in her own trade."

"So who was Rosie?" Carter asked.

"Rosie was an illustration of a woman on a recruitment poster, flexing her muscles," I replied. "The War Department found out pretty quickly that they couldn't just ask women to come forward; they had to encourage them. So they had a series of posters made that showed this woman doing the work. Since a good many of these jobs required riveting, they called her 'Rosie the Riveter.'"

"That's a cool story, Gomps," Carter said, "but what's that got to do with . . ., ah, wait a minute, were there 'Rosie's' during the Revolutionary War?"

"Yes, there were," I replied. "You got the connection."

"Of course," Hannah added, "there had to be. Men were off fighting then, too."

"True, Hannah, but with a different twist. Even though there were a women blacksmiths here and there, guns were still made by men. Some muskets were made by local gunsmiths around the colonies and others had been imported from England and France before the war, so these seemed to be in adequate supply. There weren't as many cannons as Washington needed, but factories big enough to pour the molten iron for them were few and far between, and none that we know of run by women, so the troops had to get them from battlefield victories or the French.

"It was in war supplies that we find our colonial Rosies. In addition to guns and ammunition, the troops needed equipment, food, and clothing. The trouble was that the Continental Congress and the Colonies were slow to provide money for them, if they provided it at all. Washington was constantly begging, but with little success."

"Why didn't they come up with the money?" Carter asked. "I remember from last year that they didn't, but I never understood why."

"Well, for starters, the Congress of that time had no source of money. There were no Confederation taxes, so they had to rely on the Colonies. The Colonies were in the same boat. Plus, there were many people who were still loyal to the King, and they opposed any funding. So what little money Washington got often came from the Congressmen's or officers' own pockets, such as General Nathanael Greene."

"Oh, yeah," Carter conceded, "I remember that. I guess it's just the way it had to be."

"Yup," I said, "but, sadly, that wasn't all. The officers who were in charge of supplies were not always the best we had. The best were needed at the front lines to lead the troops. So supplies were sometimes mismanaged, or worse."

"What could have been worse, Gomps?" Hannah asked.

"Corruption. A couple of the officers who were in charge of supplies lined their own pockets instead of spending the money honestly. Remember Benedict Arnold? He did that when he was managing the City of Philadelphia."

"Oh, yeah," Hannah continued. "So what about the Rosies, Gomps?"

"Yes, I should get to that, shouldn't I. There were a number of women who understood exactly what was going on. The leader of these women, at least in Philadelphia, was Esther De Berdt Reed.

⌒

"Esther was born in London in 1746 to Dennis De Berdt and his wife, whose name we don't know. They were French Huguenots who fled to England to escape religious persecution."

"What are Huguenots, Gomps?" Carter interrupted.

"Good question, Carter. Huguenots were a Christian Protestant denomination that had arisen in France. Since France was a Roman Catholic country, the Huguenots were often persecuted and driven out. Some escaped to the Colonies, if you recall."

"Oh, yeah," he replied, "I remember now — to Georgia, wasn't it?"

"Good memory," I said, "although they went to other places, too. So, the De Berdts fled to London, where Esther was born.

"The Huguenots believed that women had abilities equal to men and should be educated. Esther's father, Dennis, was no different. Esther was given an education equal to boys', and she proved to be a good student.

"Dennis had been in the import/export business in France and he continued his business in London. He did a lot of business with the American Colonies, and before long became the official English import/export agent for the Maryland and Delaware colonies.

"Sometime in Esther's late teens, a young law student from New Jersey by the name of Joseph Reed entered the picture. Reed had come to London to further his law studies and had been referred to the De Berdts by Dennis's business contacts in the colonies. The De Berdts offered Reed a place to stay while he studied in London."

"We can see what's coming," Hannah offered.

"What?" I asked.

"They fell in love," she replied. "Isn't it obvious?"

"You're absolutely right, Hannah. They wanted to marry, but Esther's father refused to allow it. Still, the two lovebirds kept up their relationship until Joseph finished his studies.

"Joseph left London for a job in Philadelphia, but he and Esther kept writing to each other. Then Joseph's father died, and Joseph returned to London. By that time, Dennis had died as well, so the last barrier to their relationship was gone.

"Esther and Joseph married in London in 1770 and immediately moved to Philadelphia. There they had six children as Joseph continued to practice law.

"Five years later, Joseph joined the Continental Army and quickly rose in the officers' ranks. Before long, he became one of General Washington's trusted assistants, along with Alexander Hamilton, Nathanael Greene and the Marquis de Lafayette. Esther remained in Philadelphia with their children — but not for long.

"Esther was one of many women who were staunch patriots. For example, in a July 22, 1775 letter to her brother she said, 'You see every person willing to sacrifice his private interest in this glorious contest. Virtue, honor, unanimity, bravery, - all conspire to carry it on, and sure it has at least a chance to be victorious. I believe it will, at last, whatever discouragements and difficulties it may meet with at first.'"

"She sounded determined," Carter said.

"No doubt," I replied, "and it was the thought of 'sacrifice' in that letter that motivated her to do what she later did. But, before I can tell you about that, we need to know more about what was going on around her.

"You may remember that, after losing the Battle of Monmouth Courthouse, the British Army disappeared, only to resurface when they came ashore south of Philadelphia. When they marched into Philadelphia, all the patriots had to get out of town, including the Continental Congress and the Reed family."

"Why did Esther have to leave?" Carter asked.

"She was a marked woman. If the British had captured her — the wife of a top assistant to Washington - she would have been held captive for ransom, at best."

"I get it," Carter acknowledged.

"So, over the next year, Esther moved the family to escape capture at least four times. These moves were expensive and very upsetting to the family.

"Finally, after the British left Philadelphia, Esther was able to move back. Undeterred by the hardships she and her family had endured, she was determined to do her part to help the revolutionary cause.

"Possibly at the suggestion of Martha Washington, whom she had known from the connection that Joseph had with George, and perhaps through her participation in Martha's wives' camps, Esther formed the Ladies Association of Philadelphia.

"Through the Ladies Association, Esther ran a campaign to raise funds aimed at easing the harsh lives of the soldiers. She organized a team of 30 women who went door-to-door in Philadelphia for donations. In a few weeks, they raised more than $7,000.00 in hard currency."

"How much would that be today, Gomps?" Carter asked.

"That's not easy to say. Because of the differences in the form of money, in the economy and in the amount of time that has passed, conversion to modern currency is almost impossible. But by all accounts, it would have been way more than $100,000.00.

"Wow!" both exclaimed. "They collected a lot of money."

"Yes, they did," I said. "At the same time, Esther wrote an essay titled 'The Sentiments of an American Woman,' in which she encouraged other colonial women to support the troops in the same way. She urged women to give up luxuries and to donate their savings. Her essay was published in just about every newspaper in the colonies, and women responded.

"Soon, Ladies Associations sprang up in other places. There was a Ladies Association of Trenton, as well as Associations in Maryland, New Jersey, and Pennsylvania. In all, they raised another $30,000."

"Wow, that was about a million!" Hannah exclaimed.

"It sure was," I concurred, "but the real story is what they did with it.

"From the beginning, Esther had openly encouraged the Congress and the colonies to give financial support to the Continental Army. She believed that they were avoiding their duty to the Revolution by failing to fund it.

"When the fund-raising by the Associations was done, Esther wrote to General Washington that she was ready to donate it to the cause. Washington wrote back that he was happy that he could put it to work where the Congress's and the colonies' funds would have gone: the day-to-day needs of the troops.

"Esther would have none of it. She wrote back, saying that if the Associations' funds were used as Washington proposed, that would let Congress and the colonies off the hook. She didn't want the Association money to substitute for money that should otherwise be government funding. She wanted the money to be used instead to make the lives of the troops easier.

"Washington insisted and Esther resisted – vehemently – in an exchange of strongly worded letters. But in the end Washington proposed a solution to which Esther agreed. The money would be used for shirts.

"Esther bought the cloth, and the Associations and other women sewed the shirts. To add a personal touch and to give the troops some reassurance that their sacrifices were appreciated, each woman sewed her name into each shirt she made."

"The first Rosie the Riveters!" Hannah exclaimed.

"Now, we get it," added Carter. "Instead of guns, they made shirts. Neat. What happened to Esther?"

"It was a sad end for her, I'm afraid. She came down with dysentery and died in 1780 at 34 years of age. She never saw the shirts completed."

"That's too bad," said Carter.

"Yeah," said Hannah. "At least she knew she had done most of it. She was tough to stand up to George Washington that way."

"Yes, she was a strong-willed person, all right," I said. "When I read the letters between them, I was amazed at how she wouldn't back down. She was determined to have the women's efforts stand for something special and not just be a substitute. I thought that the compromise was fair, although technically, government funds would have been used for shirts as well as other clothing. What clinched it for Esther, I think, was that the women could sew their names into them."

"So, Gomps, if Ester didn't live to see the shirts, who got it done?" Hannah asked.

"Believe it or not, it was Benjamin Franklin's daughter, Sarah Bache. She took over leadership and coordinated the sewing of the shirts. She was living in Philadelphia and had been a member of that Association. In the end, these 'Rosies' produced 2,200 shirts."

"Holy cow!" exclaimed Carter. "That's a lot of shirts!"

"Yes, that was a lot of shirts," I concurred, "and, Washington expressed his thanks in a letter to the Associations. In part, he said, 'The Army . . . [need not] fear that its interests will be neglected, while espoused by advocates as powerful as they are amiable.'

"And, that's it for the story of the Rosie the Riveters of the Revolution. Next time, I'll tell you about women demonstrators."

"What do you mean 'demonstrators'?" Carter asked.

"You'll see," I replied, "next week. Good night."

# 13

## STREET DEMONSTRATORS

"Gomps, you told us last year about the Sons of Liberty," Hannah began on this Wednesday, "so, was there a Daughters of Liberty?"

"Yes, Hannah, there was, although it was organized differently.

"The Sons of Liberty was a united organization of men who opposed the tyranny of the King. Groups throughout the colonies coordinated their actions and each elected or at least recognized, their own leaders, such as Sam Adams in Boston.

"The Daughters of Liberty was more of a collection of local groups of women who were all patriots and did things in opposition to the King, but were not a unified organization. Each Daughters group had its own name and its own goal, and there seems to be little evidence that the groups coordinated with one another, other than the shirt operation.

"The Ladies Association of Philadelphia was probably the closest to what the Sons of Liberty was, but they never named themselves as the Daughters of Liberty or did anything under that name.

"For example, a North Carolina woman by the name of Maude Epperson has been mentioned in history as someone who helped found the Daughters of Liberty, but there doesn't seem to be a record of what she did."

"When did it start, Gomps?" Carter asked.

"The generally accepted date is 1766, but there was no single event that kicked it off as the Boston Tea Party did for the Sons of Liberty."

"One thing the Daughters were reported to have done was to weave cloth for clothing for the Continental Army. Well, we know it was the Ladies Associations that did that. Perhaps women in other areas did the same thing, but not under a formal name.

"What we are sure of is that The Daughters of Liberty boycotted English household goods, especially clothing and tea. But rather than coming from any kind of headquarters, the boycott seems to have been called for by a variety of people throughout the colonies.

"One group that was maybe the first to boycott was called the 'Edenton Tea Party' in Edenton, North Carolina. This was a group of 51 women organized and led by Penelope Barker."

"North Carolina?" Carter interrupted.

"Yes, North Carolina. This was another example of revolutionary feeling in the South. Let me tell you about it.

"Penelope Barker was born Penelope Pagett in North Carolina in 1728. We know little of her family. She married young to John Hodges, who brought three of his own children to the marriage. Penelope and John had two more children together before he died when she was 19.

"Nineteen?" Hannah exclaimed, "She was 19 when he *died*? And they had two kids before *that*? Boy, Gomps, you were right when you said she married young."

"Yes," I continued, "but remember, that wasn't so unusual. Last year we talked about a lot of women who married young."

"I know," Hannah said, "but that made her a widow at 19, with five kids! How did she get along?"

"She married again, this time to a wealthy tobacco farmer named James Craven. Then *he* died when she was 27, and she inherited everything."

"Wait a minute, Gomps," Hannah interrupted, "Her second husband died and she was still only 27?"

"That's right."

"Did she have any kids with him?" Hannah asked.

"Not that we know of."

"Well, at least she didn't have more mouths to feed," Hannah concluded.

"Oh, I don't think she had to worry about where her next meal was coming from," I said. "James had a large plantation that was very profitable. She was his only heir, so she became wealthy overnight.

"But she apparently preferred marriage to widowhood, because she married a third time – this time to a successful businessman by the name of Thomas Barker. They lived in Edenton, North Carolina, and she had three more children with him.

"In addition to his business in North Carolina, Thomas had business interests in England and Europe and he traveled there for long periods of time. That left Penelope to manage his business and her plantation in his absence. And she became the wealthiest woman in North Carolina.

"During this time, Penelope became a strong supporter of independence for the colonies and decided to do something about it.

"Shortly after the Boston Tea Party, the North Carolina Provisional Congress had passed a Resolution in support of Boston, encouraging North Carolinians to boycott English imports, especially tea. Penelope decided to support that Resolution."

"Wait a second, Gomps," Carter interrupted, "you went too fast. What was the Provisional Congress? Wasn't this before the Revolution?"

"Good catch, Carter! North Carolina was still a colony and had an official colonial Congress in support of the King. They made laws for the colony, but the people who opposed the King wanted their own Congress. So they called it the Provisional Congress and elected their own representatives. They couldn't pass official laws, but they could oppose British rule through resolutions and petitions."

"Didn't the British try to catch them?" he continued.

"I guess they did, but like the Continental Congress when the British invaded Philadelphia, they kept moving and meeting in secret."

"Got it," he said.

"Good," I said. "So, back to Penelope Barker's story. On October 25, 1774, ten months after the Boston Tea Party, Penelope held a similar event in Edenton. She called a meeting of area women at the home of Elizabeth King, a prominent member of Edenton society.

Penelope asked them to bring all their English tea. In the meeting, she encouraged them to boycott English products . . . and to burn their tea.

"Penelope was so convincing that the group marched to the town square and set fire to their tea. In addition, they wrote a petition saying, in part, 'We, the aforesaid Ladys will not promote ye wear of any manufacturer from England until such time that all acts which tend to enslave our Native country shall be repealed.'"

"They also wrote, 'Maybe it has only been men who have protested the king up to now. That only means we women have taken too long to let our voices be heard. We are signing our names to a document, not hiding ourselves behind costumes like the men in Boston did at their tea party. The British will know who we are.' Fifty-one women signed it, and they sent it to the London newspapers."

"Whoa," Carter said, "she got a little testy with the men of Boston, didn't she?"

"Yeah," agreed Hannah. "She kind of called them weak for having disguised themselves with the Indian costumes. Those women stood up to the British and challenged the Boston men at the same time."

"They certainly did," I said. "By doing that, they marked themselves for possible harm, not only by the British Army occupying the area, but also by Loyalists who lived there.

"The English were both shocked and amused at the petition — shocked that women would carry out such a political act and amused that the women imagined that they could have any effect. One London newspaper published a political cartoon of the event, showing the Edenton women as fat, ugly, and disorganized.

"A North Carolina Loyalist, Arthur Iredell, who was living in London at the time, wrote sarcastically to his brother James, back in North Carolina, 'If the Ladies, who have ever, since the Amazonian Era, been esteem'd the most formidable Enemies, if they, I say, should attack us, the most fatal consequence is to be dreaded. So dextrous in the handling of a dart, each wound they give is mortal. . . . The more we try to conquer them, the more we are conquered.'"

"I like that, Gomps," said Hannah. 'The more we try to conquer them, the more we are conquered.' Don't mess with Amazons!"

"The funny thing is," I continued, "Iredell said it in sarcasm, but he completely misunderstood. It was a serious movement. This is another example of how out of touch the British were — and he was a North Carolinian."

"And a Loyalist," Carter added. "Same thing. But, what's an Amazon? Is that someone from the rain forest?"

"Hannah, you want to handle that one?"

"Sure, it's a mythical warrior woman. It means a woman who is big and strong. The cartoon character Wonder Woman was an Amazon."

"Got it," Carter said. "And, this guy was calling these women Amazons."

"You got it, Carter," I said. "He may have been making fun of them, but the Edenton Tea Party had the desired effect at home. The next spring, a similar gathering of women was held in Wilmington, North Carolina, and they burned tea and signed a petition, too. With that the boycott of tea and other English products by women spread throughout the colonies."

"Gomps, Massachusetts, Pennsylvania, Connecticut, South Carolina, now North Carolina," Hannah said. "There were Amazons everywhere."

"Yes, there were," I agreed, "and when it comes to public opposition to the King, there's one more I'd like to tell you about tonight. Her name was . . ."

"Ah, Gomps," Mandy interrupted, "it's getting pretty late. Can we postpone this to next week?"

"No, no, it fits right in. It's a short one."

"OK," she conceded, "but make sure it's short. I don't want you getting carried away like you sometimes do."

"I promise.

"So, her name was Hannah McDougall. She was born Hannah Bostwick, daughter of David Bostwick, pastor of the First Presbyterian Church of New York City, and his wife, whose name I don't know.

"In 1767, Hannah married Alexander McDougall, a widower and father of three children and a former merchant ship owner and privateer . . ."

"What's a privateer, again, Gomps?" Carter interrupted.

"That's a ship captain who gets a license from a country, in this case, England, to raid enemy ships at sea."

"Oh, yeah," Carter said, "you called them the first government contractors."

"That's right and they were. They got commissions to act as if they were the King's Navy, even though they were private citizens — hence the name 'privateers.'

"So, Alexander became wealthy as a privateer, but he gave up life at sea in order to settle down and tend to his family, except that to him settling down didn't mean withdrawing from public life.

"Alexander had strong feelings for independence and he became active almost immediately. He joined the New York City chapter of the Sons of Liberty and soon rose to a leadership position.

"In 1769, Alexander published anonymously an essay titled 'To The Betrayed Inhabitants' that was critical of the New York Provincial Assembly. His authorship of it was soon uncovered and he was jailed for libel, even though he never went to trial."

"They could do that?" Hannah asked.

"You mean put someone in jail without a trial?" I replied.

"Yeah."

"Yes, they could, because New York was under the control of the colonial government of the King, and their laws didn't require a trial in order to put someone in jail."

"There's another reason for the Revolution," Hannah concluded. "But what's Hannah McDougall got to do with this story?"

"You asked the right question at the right time," I said. "Hannah organized the wives of the Sons of Liberty and other women patriots, and they demonstrated."

"You mean like a street demonstration?" Carter asked.

"Exactly. They demonstrated in the streets and marched on the jail to get Alexander released. He had so many visitors that the jailers had to schedule appointments for him."

"Ha ha," the kids laughed. "Appointments for a prisoner."

"Finally, tired of all the commotion," I said, "the jailers let Alexander go. They rearrested him a few months later, but in the end, a new Provincial Governor, William Tryon, pardoned him.

"Alexander went on to a distinguished career as a Continental Army officer, and Hannah became known as the first woman street demonstrator."

"She was brave to do that," Carter observed.

"Yes, she was," I said. "And, that, Mandy, brings us to the end of tonight's story. How'd I do?"

"You did fine, Dad," she said. "You finished up just in time. And, speaking of time, it's time for these kids to get to their homework. See you next week."

# 14

## DEBORAH READ FRANKLIN

"Hi, Gomps," said Hannah, as she greeted me at the door. "We've been thinking. You've mentioned a few things about Martha Washington and some of the other wives of the Super Six. Did they do anything else?"

"Well, 'hello' to you, too," I said. "Can I sit down first?"

"Oh, sorry," she replied while following me into the house. "It's just that we've been talking about the things that all these Amazons did and we wondered if the wives of the Super Six were Amazons, too."

"I'm glad you're ready to get started tonight, but let's have some dinner first," I said. "OK?"

"Sure, Gomps," she said. "I guess I got a little ahead of myself there."

"That's OK," I said, "better than if you were bored."

After the dishes were cleared, we moved to the living room. I picked up the conversation from before dinner.

"The wives of the Super Six, eh?" I said. "Now, there's a mixture of characters. They were more different from one another, I think, than their husbands were. I'm not sure we can class them all as Amazons, but we'll meet each of them, and you can be the judge.

"First, though, let's review who the Super Six were. Do you remember?"

"Yeah," Carter said. "They were the six men who were the most important Founders of the nation, weren't they?"

"That's right," I said. "Hannah why don't you name them for us."

"Sure," she said. "Benjamin Franklin, George Washington, John Adams, Thomas Jefferson, Alexander Hamilton, and James Madison."

"Those are the ones," I said. "So, what did their wives do?"

"We'll start with Deborah Read Franklin. She was born in 1708 in England to John Read, a carpenter, and his wife Sarah. Deborah was the second of their seven children.

"Not much is known about her childhood. There is no evidence of her having gone to school, although she may have been taught to read and write at home.

"Deborah moved with her family to Philadelphia some time before 1723. They had a big house in town — big enough for their children and room to spare. They took in boarders and one of them was Benjamin Franklin.

"As you recall from last year, Benjamin had left Boston in 1723 to work for a printer in Philadelphia. That's when he rented a room from the Reads. And that's when he met Deborah.

"The attraction between Benjamin and Deborah was immediate, and in 1724 he proposed marriage to her. He was 18 and she was 16."

"Practically an old maid," Carter said.

"So, did they get married?" Hannah asked, ignoring Carter's comment.

"No, they didn't," I said. "Deborah's mother wouldn't allow it. Benjamin wasn't yet earning a steady income, and he was about to go to England on business for who knew how long. As it turned out, he got a job working for a printer in London and stayed for two years.

"Did they write to each other?" Carter asked.

"Good question, Carter," I said. "There's no evidence that they did. So as far as Deborah and her mother were concerned, Benjamin was out of the picture.

"But that left Deborah a single woman. And that's when things got interesting.

"Deborah met a man named John Rogers. We don't know much about him, but it wasn't long before they were married.

"And shortly after that, John abandoned Deborah and moved to a Caribbean island . . . with Deborah's dowry."

"That snake," Hannah said. "Did he come back?"

"Apparently not - there was no further sign of him."

"What's a dowry?" Carter asked.

"That's what parents used to give to a daughter when she gets married," I replied. "It was like giving her her inheritance early to protect her financially if her husband died. It can be money or belongings, and she can use it to start her household or just save it for a rainy day."

"Must have been a pretty big dowry for that guy to have taken off with it," Carter said.

"I guess. We don't how much, but it had to be worth a fair amount.

"Back to our story: Deborah lived at home with her parents until 1730, when, suddenly, Benjamin came back from England. He started his printing and newspaper business and it was an overnight success. And he and Deborah took up their romance again.

"Soon after, Benjamin bought a house from Deborah's parents, and they lived together as husband and wife."

". . . *as* husband and wife?" Hannah said. "That sounds like they still didn't get married."

"You're right, Hannah," I said. "They never married."

"Why not?" she continued.

"It was a matter of law. When John Rogers took off for the Caribbean, he and Deborah never got a divorce. Under the law, Deborah was still married when she and Benjamin got back together. And they didn't want to break the law."

"So how did they work it out?" Carter asked.

"They just lived together in a common-law marriage for the rest of their lives.

"Common-law marriage?" he continued. "What is that, exactly?"

"It means that they lived together *as if* they were married and after a certain number of years, they are looked upon *as* married under the law."

"They never got officially married?"

"Never officially," I said. "But they continued to live like any other married couple. And, for Deborah, that meant having two children of their own, plus raising William – Benjamin's son from a previous relationship."

"Didn't people criticize them for it?" Hannah asked.

"For living together without marrying, you mean?" I asked.

"Yeah,"

"Well, if they did, there is no evidence of it. I suspect if anyone said anything, Ben would have ignored them, maybe shot back, even. No, they seemed just to go on with their lives.

"Now, as you know from last year, Benjamin not only set up his printing business and newspaper publishing, he also set up and operated a mail delivery service that he built into the national postal service. He became the first Postmaster General.

"In 1757, Benjamin was chosen to go to England and Europe to represent the colonies and colonial businesses in import/export deals and in what amounted to international diplomacy. He became so successful that he was away from home for most of the next 30 years.

"Now, here's a question for you," I said. "With Benjamin gone for such long periods, what about his printing business, the newspaper, and the postal service?"

"He didn't sell them, did he?" Carter offered.

"You know the answer to that one from last year," I said.

"Oh, yeah," he replied, "he kept them. But couldn't they have fallen apart with no one to run them?"

"Oh, I see where you're going, Gomps," Hannah said. "Deborah ran them!"

"That's right," I said. "All the while that Benjamin was away, Deborah ran those businesses. And since he was gone for years at a time, she became what we would call today the Chief Executive Officer.

"Deborah kept the accounts, got new business, supervised the employees, maintained relations with the colonial governments, bought supplies and equipment, and had responsibility for everything."

"What about Benjamin?" Hannah asked. "Did he have any say?"

"Yes, to a limited degree," I replied. "They wrote to one another, and Deborah asked questions, and sometimes he would give her general guidance. But it often took weeks, if not months, for her to get answers, so she had to make decisions on her own. He got jobs for the print shop from Europe and he sent her the names of the people to contact, but the businesses were pretty much hers to run."

"Did she have slaves to help her, Gomps?" Carter asked. "Sounds like a lot of work."

"Benjamin had two slaves – George and King – and may have had a few others at different times. One seems to have worked in the Franklin's home and one in the print shop. Both did routine tasks. There is no record of Deborah's supervising them, but we have to assume that she did.

"Also, remember that Benjamin himself had been an indentured servant, so we also have to assume that they had indentured servants as well, especially in the print shop. Do you remember what an indentured servant is?"

"Isn't that when someone is rented out to someone else, instead of being owned?" Carter replied.

"That's exactly right, Carter. Good memory. Hannah, do you re-member how long the rental time was in those days?"

"Wasn't it about seven years?" she replied.

"That's right, too. The time depended on what the servant or the servant's family and the 'renter' agreed to do. Most of those agreements were from four to seven years.

"Of course, we know that Benjamin became increasingly uncomfort-able with the institution of slavery. He freed his slaves and became active in the anti-slavery movement, and we can assume that Deborah followed his lead, although she might have had a slave boy in her old age."

"So, who's next, Gomps?" Carter asked.

"Not so fast, Carter. There's more to the Deborah Franklin story."

"No way," he said, "more than the printing and post office?"

"That's right," I said. "Not long after they were reunited in 1730, Benjamin opened a general store in the front room of their home in Philadelphia and Deborah helped him run it.

"Over the years, they built the store into a thriving business. Maybe I should say Deborah built it. She started with writing paper and books, then added pens, ink, household supplies, medicine, tools, furniture, equipment, food, and even livestock.

"They had to expand the store to the two front rooms and later to the whole first floor. Between the print shop and the general store, there was no longer room for them to live. So, they bought another house four doors down the street and moved the family there."

"What did Deborah do in the store?" Hannah asked.

"She kept the account books, to start with," I said. "And she managed the place when Benjamin was away. Since he was away so much, that included buying the inventory, much of it through import deals, selling it, advertising . . ."

"They advertised back then?" Hannah interrupted.

"Of course," I said. "That's how they got the word out. Don't forget that they owned newspapers. The newspaper operations had to be paid for, and the price of a weekly paper was not enough to cover their costs."

"So they sold advertising," she concluded.

"They sure did," I said. "At least as much of a newspaper then was made up of advertising as it is today, maybe more. You can see copies of colonial newspapers online."

"Now, there was a time when Deborah had to become an army sergeant of sorts," I said.

"Like Molly Pitcher?" Carter asked.

"Not exactly, but close. Do you remember the Stamp Act?

"In 1765, Benjamin was in London, and while there, he tried to get the English Parliament to repeal the Stamp Act. But his political opponents in Philadelphia used his contact with Parliament to accuse him of having written the Act."

"He didn't write it, did he?" Hannah said.

"No, just the opposite, but since he was not in Philadelphia to defend himself, these people felt free to say what they wanted. They got everyone riled up, so much so that mobs threatened to set fire to the Franklins' home."

"Is this where Deborah came in?" Carter blurted.

"Exactly. Benjamin was 4,000 miles away and could do nothing. It was up to Deborah.

"The rest of their family fled across the river to New Jersey, but Deborah stayed behind to defend their property. She sent word to one of her brothers and to one of Benjamin's nephews, and together they created a fortress in the house. As she later wrote to Benjamin, 'we turned one room into a magazine. I ordered some sort of defence upstairs, such as I could manage myself.'"

"What did she mean by 'magazine,' Gomps?" Hannah asked.

"In this sense, a magazine means a storage place for guns and ammunition. They were ready to shoot it out, if need be. Luckily, the hotheads cooled off and the danger was avoided, but it sounds like she meant business."

"I call Amazon," Carter blurted.

"What?" Hannah asked.

"Gomps said we should decide if she was an Amazon," he replied, "and I'm saying she was."

"Oh, I get it," Hannah said. "Me, too. She was an Amazon, all right. What happened to her?"

"She continued to raise their family and run the businesses whenever Benjamin was away, often for years at a time," I said. "Then, around 1770, she began to have strokes. Her speech and memory got worse and worse.

"She finally died of a stroke at 66 in 1774."

"Was Benjamin there when she died?" Hannah continued.

"Sadly, no," I said. "He had been in England for a long assignment and didn't learn of her death until much later. She was buried in Philadelphia, and when Benjamin died in 1790, he was buried alongside her."

"She was tough," Carter concluded. "You've gotta say that the store and print shop and newspaper were really hers, since he was never there."

"Yeah," said Hannah, "and she did it all while raising a family and keeping a house going. She showed it could be done. Who's next?"

"Aw, you beat me to it," Carter said.

"Next time, we'll do Martha Washington," I said. "How does that sound?"

"Sounds great!" they chimed.

# 15

## THE FIRST FIRST LADY

I rang the bell, and Hannah answered the door on this Wednesday evening.

"Hi, Gomps," she chirped. "C'mon in."

"Hi, Hannah," I said. "Everyone home?"

"Oh, yes," she said. "No one wants to miss Martha Washington."

"Great," I replied, as we walked into the kitchen together. "What's for dinner? Smells good."

"One of your favorites," Mandy replied from in front of the stove. "Roast chicken with mashed potatoes and string beans."

"Yum," I said. "How soon? I'm hungry."

"Five minutes," she replied. "Everyone can sit down while I finish the potatoes."

After dinner, we sat around the living room and I began the story. "This week it's Martha Washington. We know that she was George Washington's wife, but she did a lot of living before she met him.

"Martha was born in Virginia to John and Frances Dandridge in 1731. She had three brothers and four sisters, and she was the oldest.

"The Dandridges were farmers who operated a modest 500-acre plantation that they called Chestnut Grove. Although not rich by the Virginia standards of the time, they were comfortable."

"Did they have slaves?" Hannah asked.

"Yes, probably about 20 or so. Frances inherited some land and slaves from her father and brought them into her marriage to John as a dowry. The land and slaves became part of the operation.

"What did they grow, Gomps?" Carter asked.

"Tobacco. That was still the most profitable crop in Virginia at the time.

"As a girl, Martha was schooled by her mother in the homemaking arts of the day – weaving, sewing and cooking – but she also had time for music, dancing, and horseback riding. In addition, her father made sure she got a basic education, so she learned arithmetic, reading and writing, probably along with her brothers."

"Gomps, I think you said once that most girls didn't get an education back then," Hannah said. "But it seems like a lot of the 'Amazons' did. Why is that?"

"Good question, Hannah. I'd have to say that it was mostly due to their fathers. In many cases, we have evidence that individual fathers believed that their daughters, or girls in general, could learn just as well as boys, and that education would help them just as much.

"In other cases, the girls had educated mothers who taught them. And I think some girls wanted to learn for themselves and found a way to do it. Maybe they sat in with their brothers or eavesdropped on their tutoring, or maybe they read their brothers' books in secret."

"But a lot of fathers stopped it, didn't they?" Hannah persisted.

"Yes, that was a common attitude, but apparently it didn't stop girls who were determined to learn. I imagine that there were some who had to pretend ignorance in order to cover up what they were doing."

"Huh," Hannah grunted, "I see what you mean."

"So, back to Martha," I said. "She became an attractive, skilled teenager in a well-off family — what you would call an eligible young woman. And, sure enough, she attracted the attention of Daniel Parke Custis, a wealthy plantation owner and widower who was twenty years older than she was.

"Martha and Daniel got married in 1750, when she was 18. They had four children together, two of whom died young.

"Just seven years later, Daniel died and Martha inherited everything — five plantations, including what she had brought to the marriage as dowry, and all that went with them."

"Including slaves?" Hannah asked.

"Including slaves, but we don't know how many."

"Uh, Gomps, I know that slavery is part of the history," Hannah said, "but, it's getting kinda creepy talking about inheriting human beings."

"Do you want me to stop mentioning it?"

"No, I know we have to face it, that this is what people did, but . . . I don't know," she continued. "And, I know that I've been talking about it, too. It's just that . . ."

"Carter, you bothered by it?" I asked.

"Yeah, I guess so," he replied.

"Well, you're right, Hannah, we have to include slavery in the stories where it's a part of them," I said. "In a way, we *should* be bothered by it, because it will help us to remember what a horrible practice it was.

"I have to warn you, though, slavery will become a bigger part of the story when we get to Thomas Jefferson's wife.

"So back to Martha Washington. After Daniel died, it was up to Martha to run the whole plantation, and this is where her education stood her in good stead. With the help of Daniel's business manager, she was responsible for the land, the crops, the slaves, the business deals, and the finances, along with raising the children. She even negotiated with tobacco brokers in London and with lawyers at home.

"A year or so later, she met a handsome Colonel in the Virginia Militia at a dance. His name was . . ."

"George Washington!!" the kids chimed together.

"You guessed it." I said. "They fell in love and were married in 1757. Both were 27 years old.

"George had a background much like hers — growing up on a plantation of middle size and corresponding wealth. Their marriage put them into a higher social class — together, George and Martha had vast plantation holdings and the income from a well-run operation.

"Their position in the Virginia economy required the Washingtons to entertain frequently. At the same time, George was often called away for military and government assignments. This left Martha not only to run the plantations, but also to host guests and businesspeople and to give parties.

"When the Revolutionary War broke out, we know that George was made the Commanding General of the Continental Army. He wrote frequently to Martha of the horrible conditions and the lack of Congressional funding to deal with them. This gave Martha an idea that we know as the wives' camps.

"As I've said before, Martha contacted the wives of other military officers, and they went into action. Before long, wives set up camps near each Army encampment. As the troops moved, so did the wives. And in addition to organizing them, Martha was in camp as often as the others."

"Martha herself?" Carter asked.

"Martha herself," I confirmed.

"Wasn't it dangerous?"

"The officers kept a lookout for enemy movement," I said, "and if it looked like the British might be heading in their direction, George's staff made sure the wives moved to safer places."

"And the wives were like nurses?" Carter asked.

"They were, although at first the idea was that the wives would give their husbands companionship and moral support. It soon grew to include nursing, tailoring, and cooking. It also grew to include wives of enlisted men, such as Molly Pitcher.

"By the end of the War, these camps had become an important part of the troops' lives. Even those men whose wives were not there were uplifted by the help of the wives."

"And this was Martha's idea," Hannah said.

"Not only her idea, but her doing. She took an active part in the operation."

"She had a lot of help, though, didn't she?" Carter said.

"Yes, she did, Carter, but she still made sure that everything ran smoothly, on top of doing the same for the plantations and her family."

"Amazon," Hannah said.

"Oh, yeah," seconded Carter.

"I figured that's what you'd think," I said. "Now, there's just one more thing."

"Gomps, you always say that," Hannah said.

"Don't you like it?"

"Oh, I do," she replied. "It's just that your stories always have surprises at the end."

"Well, this is not so much a surprise. It's obvious when you think about it. Let's start with a question: Who was our first President?"

"That's too easy – George Washington," Carter replied.

"Oh, and that makes Martha the first First Lady, doesn't it," Hannah said.

"Yeah," Carter added.

"See? Obvious," I said. "By this time, the War was over, so the wives' camps were disbanded, but that still left the plantations for Martha to run and family business for her to attend to.

"Now, the term 'First Lady' hadn't been adopted yet, but as the wife of the first President, Martha took on more responsibility.

"These days, our First Ladies can learn what to do from those who went before them, but just as George didn't have the actions of former Presidents to guide him in being President, Martha didn't have the actions of former First Ladies, either. Both of them had to decide from scratch what to do when and how."

"So, Martha had to figure out how to be the wife of the President," Hannah said. "You're right, Gomps, there's more to it when you look at it that way."

"There are so many things we take for granted now because they've always been done that way," I said, "but Martha had some basic decisions to make that shaped the Presidency, even to this day."

"Like what?" Carter asked.

"Here's one we take for granted," I said. "Should she live with the President in the capital, or should she stay back in Mount Vernon away from him? She decided right away to live with him.

"Here's another. Should their home be strictly living quarters for them, or should they entertain guests in it? She opened it up, even for visiting foreign dignitaries.

"Should the First Lady give advice to the President? In Martha's case, she waited for George to ask her opinion. I don't think all First Ladies have followed her lead there."

Everyone had a laugh at that.

"In the end, Martha shaped the role of the First Lady in many respects," I said. "The President's residence was treated as an extension of his office, and her experience in hosting official visitors stood her in good stead. She took responsibility for planning and supervising events of all kinds, and for greeting visitors and making them feel welcome. This became the hallmark for all First Ladies who followed her."

"You keep saying 'the President's residence,' Gomps," Carter said. "Why not just say 'the White House'?"

"Because the White House hadn't been built yet. In fact, if you remember from last year, Washington D.C. hadn't even been made the nation's capital. The first capital of our country was in Philadelphia (after a brief time in New York City), and that's where the first President's home was."

"Oh, yeah," he replied, "I remember now."

"So Martha kept up her duties as First Lady through both of George's terms as President," I continued. "And when he decided not to run for a third, they went back to Mount Vernon, where they lived out their days. George died in 1799, and Martha kept receiving visitors there right up to 1802, when she died at 70.

"Both of you said that she was one of our Amazons," I concluded, "and I don't think there's a single person who would disagree. Whether she had slaves, indentured servants, or hired help doesn't change the fact that she had the vision and the courage to see and do what needed to be done and to do it successfully and with a willing spirit. In my opinion, she deserves the place that history has given her — standing right up there next to George."

"Can't argue there," Carter said.

"Same here," Hannah added. "She was super."

"Yup," Mark said. "Martha seems to have been treated almost as an afterthought in George Washington's story. I didn't realize how big a part she played. Thanks for telling us about it. I learned a lot."

"That *was* a super story, Dad," Mandy said. "Thank you. Now, with that shining example in front of them, these two have things to do."

# 16

## THE JEFFERSON SAGA

"Tonight I'm going to tell you about Thomas Jefferson's wife, who was also named Martha," I began. "I must warn you in advance that some of this story will be unsettling, since it has to do with slaves and their relations with their owners."

"Ah, Dad, can we keep this a family hour?" Mandy asked.

"I'll do my best, Mandy, but the basics of the story can't be avoided. Let's say I'll keep it 'G' rated and no worse than 'PG.' Is that OK?"

"That's good," she said.

"Of course, now you've got our curiosities up," Mark said. "The kids aren't saying anything, but I'll bet they're ready to hear the whole thing. So, you might as well go ahead."

"OK, here goes," I said.

"Martha was the firstborn to John and Martha Eppes Wayles in Virginia in 1748."

"Gomps! How many Martha's were there in those days?" Hannah exclaimed.

"You're right, Hannah. It seems to have been a popular name. In this case, it shouldn't prove to be a problem for long."

"Why's that?" she asked.

"You'll see right now. Martha Eppes Wayles died of complications six days after giving birth to Martha, so Martha was an only child."

"Aww," Hannah said sadly.

"Martha's father, John Wayles, was a lawyer, businessman and plantation owner," I continued. "When he and Martha Eppes were married, two slaves were part of her dowry: Susanna Hemings and her eleven-year-old daughter, Elizabeth, who was called Betty. Betty was of mixed race, possibly fathered by John.

"Before they were married, John and Martha made an agreement that, when she died, Susanna and Betty would be inherited by her heirs. So, when Martha Eppes died, her daughter, Martha, inherited Susanna and Betty."

"So, Susanna and Betty Hemings were Martha's mother's slaves before she married John," Hannah said, "and they passed down to Martha when her mother died. Is that right?"

"That's right," I said.

"But, Gomps, Martha was only six days old," Carter said. "How could she have slaves?"

"Susanna and Betty were part of the Wayles household, and John probably governed them as Martha grew older."

"I see," he said, "but it isn't right that this happened."

"It seems unimaginable today," I said, "but this was how slavery was run. These kinds of situations were common throughout the Colonies at the time, as repulsive as they were.

"Getting back to the Wayles family, after his wife, Martha Eppes, died, John married twice more, both wives also dying before their time, the third, Elizabeth, in 1761.

"After Elizabeth's death, John likely took the slave Betty Hemings as his mistress, and over the next twelve years, they are said to have had six children together."

"Ahem," Mandy cleared her throat.

"I'll be careful," I said.

"Gomps, let me get this straight," Hannah interrupted. "By mistress, you mean that Betty was kind of like his wife?"

"That's what I'm trying to say, yes"

"But they weren't married," she concluded.

"They were not," I said.

"Wouldn't they be common law, whatever you call it?" Carter asked.

"Good memory, Carter," I said. "You remember Ben and Deborah Franklin."

"Yeah, like them," he continued.

"Well, I think to have a common-law marriage both people have to live *as if* they were married. I'm not sure that John wanted Betty as a wife. And I don't think the customs of that time would have accepted it."

"He just wanted the benefits," Hannah observed.

"I think that's right," I said.

"And she couldn't say no, because he owned her," Carter continued.

"Well, technically, his daughter Martha owned her," I said, "but as part of his household, no, she couldn't say no. And, to answer your next question, we don't know if either one was romantically attracted to the other — not that it mattered. He had full control over her, and that made it unfair.

"Now, as I said, John Wayles and Betty Hemings likely had six children together, and one of them was Sally Hemings."

"Not Sally Wayles," Hannah interrupted.

"Not Sally Wayles," I said.

"That tells you right there what John thought of Betty," she continued.

"I guess it does, Hannah," I said. "To continue with the story, since Betty had been inherited by Martha, all of Betty's children, including Sally, became Martha's property, too. So that was Martha's story before she married.

"In 1768 Martha Wayles married someone else before she met Thomas Jefferson. His name was Bathurst Skelton, a lawyer and distant cousin of hers."

"She married her cousin?" Carter blurted.

"Yes, Carter, cousin by marriage; not by blood. Bathurst was the brother of Martha's father's third wife! Whew, I think I got that right."

"Ha, ha, ha," everyone laughed.

"It is funny when you hear it," I said, "but the marriage didn't last. Bathurst died two years later. And, Martha's father, John Wayles, died three years after that.

"So here was Martha Wayles, a widow and orphan. At 20 years of age, with inheritances from her husband and her father, she was a very eligible young woman.

"Martha probably met Thomas Jefferson about the time of her marriage to Bathurst. Their plantations were near one another's, and plantation owners were fond of throwing parties for each other. Or, Thomas may have paid his respects to her upon the passing of her husband. In any event, Thomas fell madly in love with Martha, and the feeling was mutual.

"They married in 1772. She was 23 and a rich widow. He was 29 and a lawyer and plantation owner himself. His plantation was named Monticello.

"Martha's health was never good, and it slowly worsened as the years went by. She had diabetes and it took its toll, especially in childbirth.

"Over the next ten years, Thomas and Martha had six children together. Four died in childbirth or at a young age. Of the two who survived, one, Mary, died at 26. Only Martha, called Patsy, lived a full life, dying at 64."

"Gomps, this story has a lotta birthin' and a lotta dyin' in it," Carter observed.

"That it does, Carter," I said. "Remember that couples had big families back then. Ten, twelve children were not uncommon. But childbirth was a lot riskier for the mother than it is today, as it was for their newborns."

"Was that why they had so many children, wanting to make sure they had some left over?" Carter said.

"CARTER!" Mandy scolded.

"They didn't think about that?" he maintained. "Didn't they need kids to work their farms and all?"

"Well, maybe," she replied, "but next time try to say it in a nicer way. That was a little disrespectful."

"Sorry," he said. "It just popped out."

"In addition to the risks of childbirth," I added, "there were deadly diseases, like smallpox and dysentery, that made the average lifespan even shorter. That's probably what killed Bathurst Skelton.

"Back to Martha Jefferson. We're getting close to the end of her story, but before I finish it, I want to tell you about a few of the things that she did, because she didn't just raise a family.

"Do you remember the women who raised money for the Army shirts?"

"Yeah," Hannah said, as she paused to remember. "Wasn't one of them named Reed?"

"Right you are, Hannah! Martha Jefferson knew Martha Washington and Esther Reed, too, and she helped raise money for the shirts as well. We don't know how much, but she did.

"Also, at that time Thomas was the Governor of Virginia, and Martha served as the official hostess for him.

"Oh, and one other thing," I blurted. "I almost forgot. From the first year she moved into Monticello, she brewed beer . . ."

"Beer?" Carter interrupted amid the chuckling. "Jefferson's wife brewed beer?"

"Yes, she did. She made 170 gallons of it that first year and she continued every year until her death."

The laughter continued as Carter asked, "One hundred seventy gallons? How many six-packs would that be?"

"Hmmm . . . about a thousand," I replied.

"A thousand six-packs a year?" he said. "That's a lotta beer. Did she run a bar or did they drink it all themselves?"

"No, she didn't run a bar," I said. "It was for the whole household, but I'm sure it was for their guests and for parties, too."

"Well," he said, "that makes more sense, I guess. I pictured them stumbling around drunk all the time."

"No, I don't think that's how it was at all," I laughed. "They were sober people who just liked to enjoy themselves a little."

"And she still had her family to raise?" Hannah asked.

"Yes, Hannah, what there was of them - really only the two daughters by this time. And Martha's illnesses continued to plague her.

"Sadly, in 1782, shortly after giving birth to their sixth child, Lucy Elizabeth, Martha died. She was only 33 years old."

"Oh, no, Gomps," Hannah exclaimed, "she was so young."

"Yes, she was. She had trouble with all of her pregnancies and, with her diabetes, it seemed like it was a matter of time.

"Thomas was deeply saddened by Martha's death. He had loved her very much. For weeks afterward, he stayed in his room or went out riding alone. His daughter Patsy did her best to console him, witnessing 'many a violent outburst of grief,' in her own words.

"Before she died, Martha had asked Thomas never to marry again, and he never did, but that was part of a story that continues to this day.

"Two years after Martha died, Thomas accepted the job of Ambassador to France. He sailed to Paris with Patsy and brought along James Hemings, Sally's older brother, to be their servant.

"In 1787 Thomas sent for his younger daughter, Polly, and she brought along Sally to serve as their maid.

"Finally, they all came back to America in 1789, where both James and Sally continued to serve in Thomas's household.

"It was said that over this time, Sally had six children by Jefferson. The story created a scandal that has persisted to modern times. Some accused him of an affair with Sally even during his marriage, although there is no evidence of it. Or, you might think that he was attracted to her because she reminded him of his wife, they maybe being half-sisters."

"Half sisters?" Carter blurted. "Martha and Sally?"

"Sure," I said. "Think about it. John Wayles was Martha's father and possibly Sally's, too."

"Oh. . . yeah," Carter said, "they could have had the same father."

"Right," I said. "In 1998, Sally's descendants had blood tests done to settle the matter. The results showed that Sally's last son, Eston, was fathered by a Jefferson. Combining the history of Thomas's contact with Sally, Thomas was *possibly* the father. Some studies were done by separate researchers which show that any one of 25 male Jeffersons, nine of whom were at Monticello at the time could have been Eston's father instead, and that's where it stands today."

"Gomps, what does this have to do with Martha?" Hannah asked.

"Nothing, directly, but questions have been asked in recent years about Jefferson's relationship with his slaves and how that reflected on his character. You are likely to hear them sooner or later, so I thought I would tell the true story so you would know."

"Do you think it cuts him down as a Founder?" Carter asked.

"I don't, Carter, but Jefferson was a complicated person. When the time comes, you're going to have to decide for yourselves. I hope you'll do it on the basis of evidence and not emotion."

"That makes sense," Carter said.

"How about you, Hannah?" I asked.

"I understand what happened, I think, but, whatever I think of him, Martha did a lot."

"Was she an Amazon?" I asked.

"I'm not sure," Hannah said. "She raised a family in the middle of most of her children dying. That had to be tough. She raised money for the troops. She entertained guests and visitors as the wife of a Governor.

With her diabetes, that couldn't have been easy, but did she do anything on her own? Maybe not."

"But, she made all that beer," Carter added. "That counted for something."

"I'm with you guys," I said. "I'm not sure, either, but it doesn't hurt to count her in, I guess. And with that we'll say good night."

"Who's next, Gomps?" Carter asked.

"Elizabeth van Rensselaer Schuyler Hamilton."

"Sounds rich," he said.

"Yes, and you sound like you're stalling," I said.  "Good night."

# 17

## THE SOCIAL WORKER

"Peach!" Hannah shouted, as she opened the front door. "Hey, everybody, Peach is here."

We walked from the front door to the kitchen.

"Hi, guys," Peach said.

"Hi, Mom," Mandy said. "What brings you here?"

"Gomps thought I might know something," she replied.

"Yeah," I said. "Peach knows all about tonight's subject, so I thought she'd be the best one to tell the story."

"Great," Mark said. "Who's the subject?"

"Hi, Peach," Carter said after coming up from the basement. "Wasn't tonight going to be about that rich lady?"

"Elizabeth van Rensselaer Schuyler Hamilton," Peach said.

"So, you know about rich people?" Mark said. "More than Gomps?"

"I know more than Gomps about everything," Peach laughed.

"Ouch," I said. "Peach has a wonderful imagination, that's why she's a writer, but in this case there's more to Mrs. Hamilton than wealth."

"What else?" Hannah asked.

"It's another mystery," Peach replied, "so you're going to have to wait to find out. I'll only say that I'm not letting my 30 years as a social worker go to waste and, one of my courses in grad school was the history of social work. Now, what's for dinner? I get fed, at least, for telling this story, don't I?"

"Meat loaf, mashed potatoes and mixed vegetables," Mandy said, "and, yes, you get fed."

"Great!" she said, "so let's eat, then I'll get started.

"As we said before dinner, the subject of my story tonight is Elizabeth van Rensselaer Schuyler Hamilton," Peach began.

"Gomps told me last week that you guessed that she was rich just from the sound of her name, and you were right. Elizabeth was the daughter of Philip Schuyler, a well-known landowner and businessman, and Catherine van Rensselaer, the daughter of a wealthy Dutch family.

"Elizabeth was born in 1757 in Albany, New York, the second daughter and second of fourteen children that Philip and Catherine had together. As Elizabeth grew up, her father was elected to the New York State Assembly and as a Congressman to the Continental Congress.

"Before the Revolutionary War, Philip was made a colonel in the local militia, and when the war broke out, he resigned from the Congress and was made a major general in the Continental Army. He was planning the Battle of Saratoga when he got sick and couldn't fight at the front lines any longer. From then on, he stayed behind the lines as a battle planner and supply officer.

"Meanwhile, Catherine was busy raising her fourteen children, some say fifteen, and running their household. As you can imagine, they needed a biiiiig house for all those kids, and she had slaves and indentured servants to help her. Nonetheless, it was quite a job, including a second home north of Albany in Saratoga."

"Fourteen, fifteen kids," Hannah remarked, "I don't care how much help you have, that's a lotta work. Just the fact that she was pregnant and recovering from childbirth for at least fifteen years of their marriage must have been exhausting."

"No doubt she was tough," Peach said. "Add the hostess duties she must have had from Philip's political and military assignments, and you have one busy woman.

"So that was the family that Elizabeth was born into. The records show that she had little formal education but lots of training in sewing, cooking, and the like. She probably sat in on her brothers' tutoring while learning music and helping her mother set up for parties and houseguests.

"The turning point for Elizabeth was a trip to Morristown, New Jersey, in the winter of 1779 to visit an aunt. The Continental Army was camped nearby in their winter quarters, and one of Washington's closest assistants, Alexander Hamilton, was there."

"Was her father there?" Carter interrupted.

"Carter, that's a great question," Peach replied. "I don't know, but since he was planning strategy for the Army, he most likely was."

"Yeah, that's what I thought," he said.

"Well, that would fit in with what happened next," she continued, "because Elizabeth met Alexander Hamilton."

"Aha," Hannah said. "Maybe he heard about her and saw his chance."

"You two," Peach chided. "You're putting together a pretty interesting picture, but I'm afraid it didn't happen that way.

"You see, Alexander had been courting Elizabeth's older sister, Angelica, but she decided on another man and broke it off with Hamilton."

"So he was on the rebound?" Hannah asked.

"Looks like it," Peach replied. "He had told many of his friends that he was looking for a wife, and marrying into a family like the Schuylers would have been quite the 'coup,' as we say today. Hamilton may have thought Elizabeth was just as good a catch as her sister, and after he got to know her, maybe better.

"It wasn't long after they met that Alexander and Elizabeth got engaged. Right away, Elizabeth and her mother began planning a big wedding at their mansion."

"Wait a minute, Peach," Carter said, "Didn't Hamilton come from a broken home?"

"I think so," Peach said. "Gomps, can you fill us in?"

"Carter's right," I said. "He started out an orphan and penniless. Why do you ask, Carter?"

"Well, here's the daughter of a rich family marrying a guy from a lower class, maybe the lowest," he said. "You'd think they'd be against it."

"That's true," Peach said, "but they must have known Hamilton as a grown man, because her father was all for the marriage."

"Maybe he knew Hamilton from the Army," Carter continued.

"You know, Carter, you were onto something there, weren't you?" Peach concluded.

"A father with that much money would have fought it if he wasn't sure that the guy would fit in with the family," Carter concluded.

"Smart," Peach said. "So let's see what happened next.

"Elizabeth and Alexander were married in 1780. Over the next 22 years, they had eight children together – six boys and two girls. Four died in infancy, another died young, and three lived long lives.

"During that time, Alexander served in the Army, became a lawyer, and was Secretary of the Treasury under President George Washington.

"Elizabeth spent that time raising their family, entertaining visitors and officials, and maintaining their household. In 1800, they fulfilled their dream of building a big house, and since Alexander was away much of that time, Elizabeth took his plans and supervised the construction. They built the house in northern New York City and called it The Grange, finishing in 1802.

"Alexander was able to enjoy The Grange for only two years after it was done. As I'm sure you remember, he was killed in a duel with Aaron Burr in 1804, leaving Elizabeth a widow at 45."

"I remember that," Hannah said. "That was a sad thing."

"Yeah," said Carter, "I remember it, too. That was a mystery – how it happened."

"That's right," Peach said. "No one was ever sure if it was an accident or if Burr meant to kill him.

"At any rate, Elizabeth faced a tough time. What to do? Only three of her children were left, and only one of them was young enough to need guidance.

"We know that Elizabeth loved Alexander very much, and she wanted to defend his name against the claims of his political opponents. They even tried to disprove that Alexander had written George Washington's Farewell Address to the Continental Army."

"Why would they still accuse him if he was dead?" Hannah asked.

"He had made a lot of political enemies," Peach replied. "I think his death gave them the excuse to attack his party, the Federalists."

"Still . . ." Hannah said, her voice trailing off.

"I hear you," Peach said. "I think Elizabeth probably felt the same way. But they kept up the criticism, so she kept defending him.

"To do that, Elizabeth had to put together all his papers. With her son James, she collected everything from the house and his office, and spent years tracking down just about every document that Alexander had had anything to do with.

"One particularly important document was Alexander's draft of George Washington's Farewell Address. It turned out that the federal government had it. They wouldn't give it back, so she took them to court . . . and won!

"Elizabeth wanted to publish the papers she had gathered, but no one would do it. She asked one person after another to help her. Finally, her fifth child, John, stepped up. Over the next 30 years, John, with her help, edited and published Alexander's papers. They came to a total of seven volumes. Then he wrote his father's biography – another seven volumes.

"With this evidence, Elizabeth spent the rest of her life defending Alexander's reputation. One of his most outspoken accusers was James Monroe, who became the fifth President. Monroe had accused Alexander of corruption, and even after the evidence showed him to be innocent, Monroe continued his attack.

"Elizabeth was furious and demanded a complete apology, which Monroe refused to give. Thereafter, she refused any further contact with him. As he approached the end of his life, Monroe came to visit her and offered to apologize. She refused to accept it and turned him away."

"Wow, she was tough!" Carter remarked.

"Yes," Peach said. "You'd think that after all those years a person would lighten up a little, but not Elizabeth. Monroe had stained the name of the man she loved, and there was no forgiveness as far as she was concerned."

"That's some story," Hannah said, "but I'm not sure that makes her an Amazon. What do you think, Carter?"

"It's close," he replied, "but I didn't hear that she accomplished anything on her own. Isn't that how we're judging?"

"I think it is," Peach said. "And up to this point, you could be right. But Elizabeth's story isn't over. And the rest of it is why I'm telling it and not Gomps."

"Aha," Hannah said, "I was wondering what the connection was. So?"

"You know that I am a social worker and work with kids, right?" Peach said.

"Oh, and Elizabeth was, too?" Carter said.

"Even better," Peach replied. "After Alexander died, Elizabeth began working with other New York women to help orphaned children. They formed the New York Orphan Asylum Society in 1806 and built an orphanage. Elizabeth became the Vice President of it.

"Elizabeth worked with the children continually. In 1821, she became the President of the Society and ran the operation until 1849. By that time, she was 92 and no longer able to work."

"Ninety-two?" Hannah interrupted. "I thought people died younger in those days. And she continued working?"

"Yes, she worked all that time," Peach replied.

"Amazing," Carter observed. "Did she die then?"

"No, she didn't," Peach replied, "but she couldn't take care of herself very well, so she moved in with her daughter Eliza Hamilton Holly in Washington, D.C. She lived there five more years, dying in 1854 at 97."

"Amazon!" the kids both shouted.

"I'm with you," Peach said. "Gomps?"

"Oh, no doubt," I said. "Mandy, Mark? You go along with that?"

"Oh, yes."

"100%."

"Gomps, it just occurred to me what she lived through," Hannah said.

"Yeah, those were some tough times," I said, "especially after Alexander died."

"No, I mean what she saw through her life," Hannah corrected. "She was what? 18 when the Revolutionary War started, so she knew what was going on even before that. She lived through the war, through the Founding of the nation, through the War of 1812, and almost to the Civil War, right? She was in the middle of a lot of history."

"You're right, Hannah," Carter said. "I wonder what she thought about it all."

"We'll never know," Peach said.

"She must have left some letters or something," Carter continued. "Wouldn't they tell us?"

"I'm afraid not," Peach replied. "None of her letters to Alexander has been found. People think she burned them. We know that she was a fierce patriot and loved her country, but we don't know much about her views on the times."

"What a shame," Hannah said. "Still, she left her mark. Is that it?"

"The story, you mean?" Peach asked.

"Yeah."

"Yes, that's the end of the Elizabeth Hamilton story," Peach said. "Did you like it?"

"Yes, it was great," Hannah said. "We love your stories . . . as much as Gomps's."

"Well, on that happy note we'll say goodbye to Peach and Gomps for the night," Mandy said. "Thanks, Mom, for a great story."

# 18

## THE "PRESIDENTRESS"

"Hi, kids," I said as I walked in. "Sorry I couldn't make it last week. Duty called."

It had been two weeks since Peach and I were at the kids' house for story time. I had been away on business.

"That's OK, Gomps," Carter said, "but we had to wonder for an extra week who this story would be about."

"Well, a little curiosity never hurt," I said. "You probably narrowed it down, anyway."

"Yeah, we did," he admitted. "The last four were wives of the Super Six Founders. That would mean only Madison and Adams are left, so it has to be one of them."

"I can hardly spring a surprise anymore," I said. "You're right, it will be one of them. The Abigail Adams story is long and will take more than one night, so I'm doing Dolley Madison tonight. After that, we can take as many nights as we need to finish with Abigail."

"Everybody set?" I continued.

"Yup/yeah/sure," they chimed together.

"OK," I said. "Dolley Madison's story is a little different from the others. We know very little of her childhood and upbringing. We don't even know if she got an education.

"Dolley was born the fourth of eight children in North Carolina in 1768 to John and Mary Payne . . ."

"Thank goodness – no Martha's!" Hannah exclaimed.

"Ha, ha," I said. "Yeah, the Jefferson story was pretty hard to follow.

"Dolley was the oldest daughter among her four brothers and three sisters. Her parents had moved to North Carolina from their small plantation in Virginia. A year after her birth, they moved back."

"Why all the moving, Gomps?" Hannah asked.

"I'm not sure. The Paynes were Quakers, and a group of Quakers moved to North Carolina at that time. It's believed that the Paynes went with them, so maybe it was for religious reasons.

"In any event, in 1769 they were back at their plantation in Virginia. They lived there for 14 years. In 1783, Dolley's father freed their slaves, sold the plantation, and moved the family to Philadelphia."

"More moving," Hannah said. "There's more to that story, I bet."

"Yes, there seems to be," I said. "Quakers opposed slavery and worked to get slaves freed. That likely worked on John's and Mary's consciences. And it may be that the Paynes couldn't make their plantation profitable, either. With the price of tobacco going up and down and the costs of running a plantation, it's possible that the Paynes were simply losing money.

"Once in Philadelphia, John started a laundry starch– making business," I continued, "but he went broke at that six years later. Maybe he just wasn't a good businessman.

"The one good thing to come out of this time was Dolley's marriage to John Todd. He was a lawyer of Quaker faith with a modest practice in Philadelphia. After a short courtship, they were married in 1790, and she moved into his home. They had two children – both boys – Payne and William.

"Two years later, Dolley's father died. Her mother and the rest of the family were left penniless. To make ends meet, Mary turned their Philadelphia home into a boarding house, and during that time, Aaron Burr was a boarder there . . ."

"The guy that shot Hamilton?" Carter blurted.

"Yes, Carter, that guy. And he'll come back into our story in a minute.

"Sadly, Dolley's mother couldn't make a go of it in the boarding house business, and in 1793 she moved in with another daughter, Lucy, in West Virginia.

"1793 turned out not to be a good year for their families," I said. "In addition to the failure of Mary's boarding house, an epidemic of yellow fever broke out across Philadelphia. Over 5,000 people died in four months, including Dolley's husband, John Todd, and their younger son, William. She was a widow at 25 with no money and her son, Payne, to raise."

"Couldn't she move in with John's parents?" Hannah asked.

"It would have been a good idea, but they had died of yellow fever, too."

"Oh, no," she gasped, "both of them?"

"Yes," I replied. "At this point, she really had no one . . . until luck finally came her way.

"Remember that Aaron Burr had rented a room at their boarding house?"

"Yeah?" Carter said.

"Well, he did at least one good deed in his life. He introduced Dolley to James Madison."

"How odd," Hannah observed. "There's gotta be a story behind that."

"Yes, there is," I said. "It turns out that Burr and Madison knew each other from college – they both went to Princeton – and from the House of Representatives, where they were both Congressmen.

"By the time of his meeting Dolley, Madison was 43 years old and had never married. Most thought he was well past the age when he would be thought of as an eligible bachelor."

"Why didn't he get married before?" Carter asked.

"Good question," I replied. "Remember that he was frail and sickly all his life, and it seemed like he spent what energy he had on founding our nation. The little he had left over went to keeping his plantation, Montpelier, going. And, he just hadn't seemed to click with any of the women he had met.

"Madison seems to have given up hope, but his friends had not. They could see what he couldn't – that a loving wife would make his life better. Aaron Burr saw in Dolley the perfect match for James.

"In spite of their age difference, James and Dolley took to one another right away. They had a short courtship and were married the next year – 1794. One of the first things James did was to adopt Dolley's son, Payne, and with that Dolley's future was set.

"Three years later, James left Congress to return to Montpelier and devote more of his time to farming. He brought Dolley and Payne with him, of course, and they helped him to bring his operation out of the debt he had gotten into because of his devotion to Congress.

"But that lasted only three years. James's friend Thomas Jefferson was elected President in 1800, and one of his first acts was to ask James to be his Secretary of State. James jumped at the chance. Politics was in his blood.

"By this time, the national capital had been moved to Washington, D.C., and the Madison family moved there so that James could take up his post. It wasn't long before Dolley discovered that politics was in her blood, too.

"As part of his job as Secretary of State, James had to host receptions and dinners for diplomats of other countries. Dolley saw the importance of these events as a chance to persuade their guests to side with the United States. So while she was running the parties, she was paying attention to the guests, too.

"James and Thomas Jefferson saw how successful these dinners were. Dolley charmed the visitors with her sparkling personality while putting pressure on them to agree to James and Thomas's way of think-ing. She made it hard for them to say no.

"Jefferson, of course, was a widower by this time and had no one to serve as his First Lady. In fact, the concept of the First Lady as an informal diplomat had not yet been formed."

"What about Martha Washington?" Hannah asked.

"That's another good question, Hannah. Through parties and per-sonal relations, Martha made visitors feel comfortable and open to dis-cussing politics, but she did not serve as an advocate of the President's policies.

"Enter Dolley Madison. Jefferson understood how important Dolley could be to his efforts, so he often called upon her to serve as his hostess for these official events as well as to greet public visitors. The role of 'First Lady' was complete.

"At the same time, the expansion of the White House had begun. The architect for it was Benjamin Henry Latrobe. Dolley saw the need for a 'First Lady's' hand in the design and furnishing of the new spaces, so she just went right ahead and consulted with Latrobe until it was done.

"Dolley continued in her relationship with Jefferson through both of his terms of office. Some newspapers called her the 'Presidentress,' and the public fell in love with her. When Jefferson chose not to run af-ter his second term, James was elected to succeed him. No one doubted that Dolley's popularity helped him to victory.

"James took office as President in 1809, and Dolley picked up right where she had left off with Jefferson. She planned and hosted events and greeted visitors of all kinds to the White House. Dolley cemented the importance of the President's wife in the advancement of our nation's interests.

"Dolley's last chapter was an act of bravery over which some historians disagree. James was elected to his second Presidential term at the same time that the War of 1812 with England broke out. Two years later, British forces invaded Washington, D.C. and were burning it."

"The British attacked Washington?" Carter exclaimed.

"That's right," I said. "They overpowered our forces and marched right into the City."

"Didn't we just beat them in the Revolution?"

"Yes, Carter, but remember that they were still a world power and didn't want some upstart country standing in their way.

"So, everyone fled the White House except Dolley and a few friends," I continued. "She insisted on staying behind until a priceless painting of George Washington could be unscrewed from its place on a wall and carried to safety."

"Did they make it?" Carter asked.

"Yes, they escaped, with the painting."

"What's the argument about?" he continued.

"Some say she took down the painting herself," I said, "and others say she just ordered it taken down and that her friends did it."

"That's it?" he said.

"Apparently so."

"Big deal!" he said. "She stayed behind to make sure it got done, right? Who cares who actually took it down?"

"Not me," I said. "But if it makes any difference to you, she said in a letter retelling the moment, 'I have ordered the frame to be broken and the canvas to be taken out . . . It is done.' A few days later, the British left Washington, everyone went back to the city, and Dolley returned the painting to its place with a new frame.

"James's second presidential term was up two years later, and he decided to leave public life and return to Montpelier. There they lived, trying to make a go of it, until James died in 1836. By that time, he had large debts, and Dolley was left with them."

"He owned a plantation, didn't he, Gomps?" Hannah asked. "I thought he was rich."

"No, Hannah, he wasn't," I said. "As I've said, it took good business skills to make a plantation profitable, and not everyone could do it."

"Even with slaves?" she continued.

"Even with slaves," I said. "It was expensive to maintain them. Add to that the changes in the prices for tobacco and other crops, and you have a business that takes daily attention to keep afloat. James had been away from Montpelier for years at a time.

"On top of that, James had a particular problem that added to his debt. Dolley's son, Payne, whom he had adopted, was never able to keep a job. He was addicted to alcohol and gambling. He ran up big debts in his father's name, and James, to his everlasting credit, took on those debts as his own.

"So when James died, the debts became Dolley's. After a year living in Montpelier, she moved in with her niece, Anna, in a row house James owned in Washington D.C. There she spent her days gathering James's papers and copying them. She ended up with seven volumes of documents and tried to sell them to Congress to pay off the debts. Congress delayed.

"With no other source of income, Dolley was forced to sell Montpelier. She used the money to pay off the last of the debts.

"Still living in Anna's home, in poverty, Dolley finally convinced Congress to buy James's papers. In 1848, they agreed to pay her $22,000 for them, probably about $300,000.

"A year later, Dolley died at home at the age of 81. Although never in an official job, she had served her country long and well.

"So, what do you think, was she an Amazon?" I asked.

"I think so," Hannah replied. "She went through a lot."

"What do you think, Carter?" I asked.

"I think so, too," he said. "She didn't create anything or run a business like the others, but she showed how First Ladies after her could help the President. She was kinda like George Washington. He had to invent what a President *should* do and she invented what a First Lady *could* do."

"Well, that's quite the observation," I said. "I think that's a fitting way to end her story."

# 19

## ABIGAIL ADAMS

"The last of the wives of the Super Six Founders is Abigail Adams," I began on this night. "You may have heard of her. She was the wife of John Adams who was our second President, first Vice President and a key diplomat during the Revolutionary War. He relied heavily on Abigail for advice."

"Even when he was President?" Hannah asked.

"Oh, yes," I replied, "probably from when they first married. Certainly during his time in Congress and as an ambassador."

"Didn't he get mad?" she continued.

"There were times when he seemed to, but he knew that she understood people better than he did, so he put up with it."

"How do you know all this, Gomps?" Carter asked.

"It seems like that's pretty detailed stuff to know from 250 years ago. Is that what you're asking?"

"Yeah," he replied.

"Don't tell us," Hannah answered. "They wrote it down and kept it."

"That's right, Hannah. Abigail and John wrote letters to one another throughout their marriage, and even before. And they wrote to a lot of other people, too. Many of the letters have been saved and published, so we can read them today. But, before we can talk about the letters, we need to learn more about Abigail."

"Abigail was born in 1744 to William Smith, a Puritan minister, and Elizabeth Quincy Smith in Weymouth, Massachusetts. She was the second of three daughters and one son. Her early years were spent learning her three R's, as well as dancing and sewing, at home and on extended visits to her grandparents.

"Being a Puritan, William believed that girls should be educated. As in many other Puritan families, their mother taught the girls at home and William gave them complete run of his library."

"It was in that library that Abigail read and learned. From the Greek philosophers to Shakespeare and the English poet John Milton, she immersed herself in books."

"How did they meet?" Hannah asked.

"John and Abigail?" I asked.

"Yeah."

"They were third cousins by marriage. John and Abigail lived near one another while growing up and they knew each other from family gatherings. Then, they went their separate ways and didn't see each other for a few years.

"When Abigail was 17, a friend of John's by the name of Richard Cranch was courting her older sister, Mary. On one of his visits to see her, Cranch brought John along, and Adams took a liking to Abigail.

"Though shy, Abigail had long conversations with John about politics, literature, religion, and child-raising. The more they talked the more they fell in love, although no one would take either of them for romantic people."

"Why not, Gomps?" Hannah asked.

"They were both descended from Puritan stock," I replied. "They had stern personalities and Puritan values — hard work, belief in God, prudence, thrift, and restraint.

"At one point, Abigail, apparently impressed with John's maturity and experience, wrote to him asking for his honest opinion of her. He wrote back with what today seems like brutal honesty, telling her, in advance, 'to resolve upon a Reformation [of yourself].'"

"What did he mean by that?" Hannah asked.

"That she should promise to improve herself in the ways he recommended," I replied. "He criticized her for failing to play cards. He criticized her for blushing in public, as a 'Violation of Decency.' He criticized her for never having learned to sing, for failing to sit up straight, for sitting cross-legged, and for walking with her toes pointed in — pigeon-toed."

"Are you kidding?" Hannah said. "What a jerk!"

"Hannah!" Mandy said.

"Sorry," she replied, "but, how judgmental!"

"She asked," Carter said.

"Yeah, I guess," Hannah admitted. "But, how could she stand him?"

"You'd think that she would have ended it for that alone," I said, "but it was just the opposite. In a return letter, she said how much she appreciated knowing what faults she could correct.

"Now, I'm going to turn the tables on you. Some say that John wrote that letter as a joke. They say that he thought her to be so perfect that he could only cite ridiculous things – things said only in jest."

"Like what, Gomps?" Hannah asked.

"Well, I'll quote part of his letter for you and you can be the judge.

"'. . . In the Fourth Place you very often hang your Head like a Bulrush. You do not sit, erected as you ought, by which Means, it happens that you appear too short for a Beauty, and the Company looses the sweet smiles of that Countenance and the bright sparkles of those Eyes. - This Fault is the Effect and Consequence of another, still more inexcusable in a Lady. I mean an Habit of Reading, Writing and Thinking. -- But both the Cause and the Effect ought to be repented and amended as soon as possible. ...'"

"I think he was joking," Hannah concluded. "Sounds like he was praising her."

"Same here," Carter added, "but it seems like a strange way to do it. Did she correct him, too?" Carter asked.

"For the rest of his life," I replied, to everyone's amusement.

"This odd couple waited only six more months before marrying. Abigail's mother objected, but her opposition couldn't stand up to them. The wedding took place on October 25, 1764. Abigail was 19 and John was just turning 29.

"Right after the wedding, the newlyweds got on a horse together and rode to his farm in Braintree, Massachusetts . . ."

"No honeymoon?" Hannah interrupted.

"No, Hannah, honeymoons were unknown for average people at the time. Most newlyweds had too much to do."

"What kind of farm did he have?" Carter asked.

"It wasn't much of a farm, especially by southern standards. It had a small farmhouse, a barn, and 40 acres of land. But Abigail turned the place into a home, and they proceeded to make a go of it there.

"I should say that Abigail made a go of it. John was a country lawyer. He rode from town to town, taking cases in local courts. They called that 'circuit riding' and it meant that he was seldom home.

"That left Abigail alone a good part of the time, so it was up to her to handle everything. She cooked, cleaned, sewed, and kept track of the family finances. She grew a vegetable garden and ran the farm.

"OK," Carter interrupted, "but if John was away all the time, who did the plowing?"

"Good question, Carter. That's where things got complicated. Abigail couldn't handle that sort of thing herself. She hired farm hands to help her with the plowing and livestock, and she rented out the fields to tenant farmers."

"How many farmers?" Carter asked.

"As many as six tenants at one time and usually three or four hired hands," I said.

"And she knew how to run all that?" he continued.

"Probably more than John thought. He told her what to do in his frequent letters to her. And she tried to follow his instructions, but things were not as easy as John made them out to be, so she often had to make her own decisions.

"Didn't she get mad, being told what to do?" Hannah asked.

"Apparently not," I replied. "She usually wrote back telling him how she had carried out his instructions."

"Were the letters just about telling her what to do?" Hannah asked.

"Not hardly," I said. "They wrote about everything you could imagine: their love for each other, family news, personal business and finances, friends' activities, current events, politics, philosophy, religion, forms of government, even women's rights."

"What were the letters like?" Hannah asked.

"Take their love letters," I said. "Early in their relationship John wrote to her as he traveled the circuit, 'Oh, my dear girl, I thank Heaven that another Fortnight will restore you to me – after so long a separation.'"

"What's a fortnight, Gomps?" Carter asked.

"Fourteen nights. He meant that he would be home in two weeks.

"At different times, he called her pet names like 'Miss Adorable' 'My Dear,' 'My Dearest Friend,' or 'Diana,' after the Greek Goddess.

"Abigail sent John love notes of her own. During his first trip to Philadelphia, in 1774, she wrote, 'I dare not Express to you at 300 hundred miles distance how ardently I long for your return. I have some very miserly Wishes; and cannot consent to your spending one hour in Town till at least I have had you 12.'"

"Hm, pretty steamy," Hannah said.

"Well, they did have six children," I said.

Everyone chuckled at that.

"So she had six kids to raise, on top of everything else," Carter said.

"Oh, we're just getting started with what Abigail did," I said. "As John traveled, he probably bragged to his friends about her. She was so impressive that an English visitor wrote to John Adams of Abigail that she 'was the most accomplished Lady I have seen since I came out of England.'"

Before long, she was carrying on regular correspondence with all the major Founding Fathers and their wives – Washington, Jefferson, Madison - with other members of the Continental Congress, and with someone who would become perhaps her best friend - Mercy Otis Warren."

"Who was that, Gomps?" Hannah asked. "I've never heard of her. Have you, Carter?"

"Nope."

"Mercy Otis Warren was a key person in the Founding story," I said. "Most people haven't heard of her, but her story is fascinating and I'll tell it next time.

"Back to Abigail. She reported to her correspondents what she had seen and heard as she traveled around the Boston area. In turn, they asked for her opinions on the Revolution, foreign policy, the Constitution, and many other subjects of the nation's Founding.

"As John built his law business, he decided that he could get more clients if he had an office in Boston. So, in 1768, he and Abigail scouted around and rented a house – the 'White House' – on Brattle Square. Soon after they moved in, however, British troops moved into the neighborhood, too, and John and Abigail found it dangerous, especially for the children.

"A year later, they moved to Colt Lane, in a safer part of town. That house proved unsuitable, though, so they moved back to the White House after several months.

"By this time, John had been elected to the General Court, so he had his law practice and his duties as a representative to the Court. He was a busy man, so busy that it seemed to have a bad effect on his health. In hopes that the country air would help him feel better, they moved back to the farm in Braintree, keeping his office in the White House."

"Gomps, it sounds like they did a lot of moving," Hannah said. "How much of it did Abigail do?"

"Probably all of it," I replied, "at least all of the planning and supervising. By this time John was making a good living, so they had servants to help move them, but with three children, she had her hands full."

"It sounds like it," she said.

"It didn't end there, either," I said. "Although John's health improved, thanks in no small part to his trips to Stafford Springs, Connecticut, to take the mineral spring waters, John was faced with what we would think of as commuting to work. Having to go back and forth to Boston put another kind of strain on him, so, again, they faced the need to live in Boston.

"After a short search, John and Abigail found a brick house on South Queen Street between the courthouse and the White House. They bought it in August, 1772, and moved in on November 24."

"Why so long, Gomps?" Carter asked.

"You mean between buying and moving in?"

"Yeah."

"Abigail was eight months pregnant when they bought the Queen Street house. She decided to have the baby in a familiar place - the farm. The child, Thomas, was born in September and they waited until he was two months old before moving to the brick house. That also gave them time to get it ready. At the same time, she had met Mercy Otis Warren and had struck up the correspondence with her.

"The Queen Street house gave Abigail the chance to see the buildup of British troops and the growing opposition of the Boston patriots. She reported on all this by letter to Mercy, who begged her for 'very long letters' with all the information she could give. After John left for the Continental Congress, Abigail began her reports to him and, later, to other Founders, including Elbridge Gerry, a signer of the Declaration of Independence, a member of the Massachusetts and Continental Congresses and a person who would play a key part in Abigail's relationship with Mercy Otis Warren.

"After the Sons of Liberty dumped the tea in Boston Harbor during the Boston Tea Party, Abigail wrote to Mercy that she was relieved

that at least no blood had been spilled, but she feared the results of the
formation of two sides, 'factions' she called them, within the colonists.
The two sides were the Tories and Whigs - those loyal to the King and
those in favor of independence."

"Were those like political parties, Gomps?" Hannah asked.

"The Tories and Whigs?"

"Yeah."

"That's exactly what they were.

"To John, in Philadelphia, Abigail wrote, '. . . there is nothing more
shameful and at the same time more pernicious when [peace is] attained
by bad measures, and purchased at the price of liberty.'"

"What did she mean by that?" Carter asked.

"That it is ruinous to a people to give up their freedoms in trade for
peace," I replied. "In the same letter, she said, 'Did ever any Kingdom
or State regain their Liberty, when once it was invaded without Blood
Shed?' Meaning that a country that has been invaded must fight to kick
out the invaders; they will not leave just through negotiations.

"Those are the kinds of opinions that Abigail gave to all her correspondents on a regular basis, in addition to her reports of what was
happening. In fact, as the Revolutionary War began, she wrote one of
her most famous letters to John, assuming he would have a hand in
drawing up new laws: 'I long to hear that you have declared an inde-
pendency – and by the way in the New Code of Laws which I suppose
it will be necessary for you to make I desire you would Remember the
Ladies, and be more generous and favourable to them than your ances-
tors. Do not put such unlimited power into the hands of the Husbands.

Remember all Men would be tyrants if they could. If perticuliar care and attention is not paid to the Laidies we are determined to foment a Rebelion, and will not hold ourselves bound by any Laws in which we have no voice, or Representation.'"

"Holy cow!" exclaimed Hannah. "She wanted a second revolution - of women against men! She didn't mess around! Did he answer her?"

"Yes, he did. In his next letter and he gave no ground. He wrote, 'Altho they [powers of the men] are in full Force, you know they are little more than Theory . . . in Practice you know we are the subjects. We have only the Name of Masters, and rather than give up this, which would compleatly subject Us to the Despotism of the Peticoat, I hope General Washington, and all our brave Heroes would fight.'"

"Meaning?"

"Meaning that in reality, women already ruled, through what he called 'the Despotism of the Peticoat,' and that she could expect the men to stand up for themselves. In effect, he was dismissing her demands.

"She didn't give up, though," I continued, "and from time to time in her later letters she brought it up again. In one, she wrote, 'I can not say that I think you very generous to the Ladies, for whilst you are proclaiming peace and good will in Men, Emancipating all Nations, you insist upon retaining an absolute power over wives. But you must remember that . . . we have it in our power not only to free ourselves but to subdue our Masters, and without violence throw both your natural and legal authority at our feet.'

"Thinking that she had gone too far, Abigail started her next letter with a peace offering. She wrote, 'I set down to write you a Letter wholly Domestick with out one word of politicks or any thing of the Kind, and tho you may have matters of infinately more importance before you, let it come as a relaxation to you.' And with that, she proceeded to write several hundred words on family matters, farm and personal business, and current events."

"How did he take this?" Hannah asked.

"Well, I think John really liked having a smart wife, but there were times when he wished she wasn't so assertive. He wanted her opinions, but maybe only when he wanted them.

"In his next letter to her, he tried to smooth things out, but couldn't help reminding her that she was his wife and therefore subordinate to him, writing, 'Your Sentiments of the Duties We owe to our Country, are such as become the best of Women, and the best of Men . . . nothing has contributed so much to support my Mind, as the choice Blessing of a Wife, whose Capacity, enabled her to comprehend, and whose pure Virtue obliged her to approve the Views of her Husband.'

"Then, he asked for peace between them by saying, 'I want to take a Walk with you in the Garden – to go over to the Common – the Plain – the Meadow.'"

"Did it work?" Carter asked.

"It seems to have, Carter, although the mail delivery could have had a hand in it. Abigail didn't get John's next few letters for several weeks. By the time they had arrived, the Declaration of Independence had been signed, and that seems to have given them something more immediate to talk about. At the same time, Abigail had an eye infection and couldn't write.

"Over the next year, John traveled back and forth between Braintree and Philadelphia, taking leaves from Congress to spend time with his family. In November, 1777, he was appointed as a diplomat to France. This began a long series of assignments to Europe and England in one diplomatic role after another, usually for years at a time. It was up to Abigail to manage everything.

"John's absences increased the need for their letter writing. John reported his activities in Paris and asked for her opinions on his plans for diplomacy. She reported the current events from the colonies, gave him political advice, and asked for . . . ribbon."

"Ribbon?" Hannah exclaimed. "Why ribbon?"

"Well, the boycott of English goods had forced the colonists to dress very plainly. Abigail wanted a little French ribbon to dress up her clothes, so she asked John for some, and he bought it for her. Then, she asked for thread and lace. He bought those and sent them. Then, she asked for buttons and cloth. He bought those, too.

"Seeing that Abigail's dresses were getting a little fancy, her friends and neighbors asked her about it. When she told them, they wanted to do the same. Out came Abigail's pen.

"Before long, John was supplying Abigail with sewing goods on a regular basis, and she was bartering and selling them. She was building a little sewing supplies business, what they called 'notions' in those days, and she was keeping John busy forwarding her orders to her suppliers.

"Finally, John had had enough. In a letter, he told her that instead of sending her orders to him, she should order directly from the manufacturers, whose names and addresses he included. Abigail wrote back, thanking him and accepting his suggestion. She had her own retail business."

"In the midst of everything else," Hannah said.

"In the midst of everything else," I confirmed.

"Managing the farm and raising the kids."

"Yup."

"Advising John and writing to all those people."

"Yup."

"Anything else?"

"Anything else, what?" I asked.

"Did she do anything else all this time?" Hannah asked.

"She did, Hannah, but, we're going to have to start that story next time."

# 20

## THE SCRIBBLER

"Tonight, you're going to get to know Mercy Otis Warren," I said. "I've mentioned her before and now it's time for you to meet her."

❧

"Mercy Otis Warren was born in 1728 to Colonel James Otis and his wife Mary in West Barnstable, Massachusetts."

"Is that on Cape Cod?" Carter asked.

"Yes, it is, Carter, kind of in the middle.

"Mercy was the third born of 13 children . . ."

"Wow – another big family!" Hannah interrupted.

". . . and the first daughter," I continued.

"Mercy's mother was a direct descendant of Edward Doty, a passenger on the Mayflower. Her father was a lawyer, a judge, and was elected to the Massachusetts Assembly, so she was right in the middle of government business.

"They lived on a farm that Mary ran when James was away on business, which was often."

"She ran a farm and raised 13 kids?" Carter asked.

"Yes, she did."

"There's an Amazon, right there," he declared.

"For sure," Hannah added.

"James was an independent kind of guy," I continued. "He didn't like being told what to do. So when the Governor sent troops around the Colony to enforce the collection of taxes, James complained.

"Before long, James was speaking publicly against colonial oppression. Mercy and her brothers and sisters heard him and no doubt it affected their thinking."

"What about school?" Hannah asked. "Did she go?"

"No, Mercy had no formal education. Her brothers didn't either; they were tutored privately by a local minister. He must have been a pretty good teacher because Mercy's brother James, or Jemmy as he was called, went on to attend Harvard College.

"One day, Joseph, Mercy's oldest brother, decided he didn't want to go to college and dropped out of the tutoring. Mercy saw her chance and sat in on the sessions in his place. That's how she learned her three R's.

"Mercy took to her studies instantly. She read Greek, Latin, French, and English literature, history and philosophy. Among her favorites was Sir Walter Raleigh's *History of the World*."

"Wasn't he the guy who sent the first ship to America?" Hannah asked.

"Wow, Hannah, you've got some memory," I said. "Yes, Raleigh was the one who put that first voyage together.

"So, from all that reading, a love of learning grew in Mercy, especially of political history. And, from that, she put together her own thoughts about people's rights, including the rights of women. At first, she accepted a more traditional women's role, referring to it as the 'weak and timid sex.' But, as time went on, she demanded increasingly that women gain equality, in everything.

"In 1743 Mercy went to Jemmy's graduation from Harvard. There she met Jemmy's classmate James Warren, of nearby Plymouth, Massachusetts.

"Mercy and James Warren took up a long courtship and were finally married eleven years later. She moved in with him at his family farm in Plymouth and over the next twelve years, they had five children – all boys. She settled down to what she thought, at the time, would be life as a homemaker and mother.

"As for James Warren, he was already a part of Plymouth public life when Mercy married him. His father was the High Sheriff of the county, and James took on the job just two years after the wedding. In 1765, he was elected to the Massachusetts Assembly, where he became Speaker of the House and President of the Provincial Congress. And, like Mercy's father and her brother Jemmy, James Warren became an opponent of English rule of the colonies.

"Mercy and James Warren were devoted to each other and, from the beginning, expressed it in frequent love letters when he was away. He called her the 'scribbler,' and in writing those letters she probably discovered an ability to put her thoughts into words.

"James encouraged Mercy to write, and her simple letters evolved into poems, plays, essays, and reports of current events, especially of wartime conditions. And he depended on her opinions of current events.

"Mercy began writing poems at least as early as 1759, when she wrote 'On Winter,' in praise of the return of spring in Plymouth. Other poems soon followed, along with her plays and essays, all published anonymously until 1790."

"Why anonymously, Gomps?" Hannah asked.

"Mercy was quite reluctant, as a woman, to expose her writing to public criticism, especially to that of men. She believed that their beliefs about women — that they were inferior, intellectually — would deny her a fair reading."

"But she was right, wasn't she, Gomps?" Hannah added.

"Among society as a whole, yes, but not according to those who knew her. They were some of the most important men of the Revolution — her father, her brother, her husband, George Washington, Thomas Jefferson, Samuel Adams, John Hancock, Patrick Henry, and most of all, John Adams."

"Wow," she continued. "She wrote to all of them?"

"Yes, and they wrote back.

"It was John Adams who wrote to Mercy's husband, 'Tell your wife that God Almighty has entrusted her with the Powers for the good of the World, which, in the cause of his Providence, he bestows on few of the human race. That instead of being a fault to use them, it would be criminal to neglect them.'"

"Meaning that she had writing ability and that it would be a crime not to use it?" Carter said.

"I couldn't have put it better," I replied. "Ability to write *and* think."

"How did John Adams know about Mercy, if she was just a house-wife?" Carter asked.

"Ah, that's where this story gets interesting. The Adams and Warren families became intertwined starting in 1761. It was on February 24 of that year that Mercy's brother Jemmy appeared before the Massachusetts Superior Court to protest the Writs of Assistance – a British law in the colonies that allowed troops to enter and search houses without a search warrant. John Adams was in the audience, taking notes.

"By this time, Jemmy was a noted lawyer and an outspoken sup-porter of independence for the colonies. He spoke for four hours that day in opposition to the Writs, and to British domination of the colo-nies. In his argument, he spoke the famous saying, 'Taxation without representation is tyranny.'"

"I've heard that before!" Hannah exclaimed. "Is that the first time it was said?"

"Hannah, that's a good question. The Founders took it to be the first time, and they used it as a rallying cry. In fact, Jemmy became fa-mous for saying it, but he wasn't the first. That statement had been made in Ireland some 30 years before in *their* cause against England. How Jemmy knew of it, we have no idea.

"But news of Jemmy's speech spread far and wide in Massachusetts, so much so that in the next election, he was voted into the Massachusetts Assembly.

"Moved by Jemmy's argument before the Court, John Adams turned his notes on the speech into a report of his own, and, together with Jemmy's famous quote, it became a powerful argument for independence.

"Mercy heard about Jemmy's speech, too, and it seemed to be the spark that changed her from quiet housewife to outspoken patriot. Her home became a meeting place for the Sons of Liberty and other political groups. John Adams visited many times, writing to Abigail in 1767 that 'In Col. Warren and his lady I find friends.'"

"It sounds like Mercy still hadn't met Abigail," Hannah said. "Is that right?"

"Yes, it is. John wrote to Abigail of his meetings with them, but she did not meet them until six years after that letter."

"How odd," Carter observed. "Didn't they live near each other?"

"Wow, Carter, you've been studying your geography. Yes, the Adamses lived in Braintree, only 30 miles from the Warrens in Plymouth."

"You'd think they'd have gotten together sooner," he continued.

"You'd think," I said. "To me it shows how occupied Abigail and Mercy were with raising their families and running their households.

"At that first meeting, though, the two couples hit it off, and Mercy wrote to Abigail shortly after. That started a lifetime of relationship through letters and visits that strengthened their roles in our nation's Founding."

"So, now you've got the early history of Mercy," I said. "That's a good stopping point for tonight. I've got some prep work to do for tomorrow's business trip, so I'll say good night."

# 21

## A FRIENDSHIP BLOSSOMS

On the following Wednesday, I began our session. "Abigail Adams had just met James and Mercy Warren. When John had gone to Plymouth on one of his circuit riding trips, Abigail went along.

"Despite there being sixteen years' difference in their ages, Abigail and Mercy struck up a friendship right away. After the trip, Mercy wrote to Abigail telling her how much she enjoyed the visit. Abigail wrote back as if they had been lifelong friends, asking Mercy for her opinions on child-raising.

"Over the next 30 years, Mercy and Abigail exchanged ideas and opinions about every aspect of the Revolution and the new nation. And they encouraged one another to exert their influence as well.

"One example was inspired by the Boston Tea Party. Shortly after, Abigail wrote to Mercy that she feared that peace between England and the Colonies would be lost, saying, '. . . if once they are made desperate Many, very Many of our Heroes will spend their lives in the cause, With the Speach of Cato in their Mouths, 'What a pitty it is, that we can die but once to save our Country.'"

"Wait a minute, Gomps," Carter said. "Didn't somebody else say something like that?"

"You're quick. Yes, Nathan Hale said that before he was hanged as a spy: 'I regret that I have but one life to give for my country.'"

"Was that after this?"

"Yes, it was – during the Revolutionary War."

"So, Nathan Hale wasn't the first to say it," Carter continued.

"No, he wasn't," I said.

"Abigail was?"

"No, she wasn't either. The historians think that the Roman statesman Cato said it first. In fact, Abigail credited him in her letter when she said, 'With the Speach of Cato in their Mouths . . .'"

"Aha," Carter said. "But Nathan Hale did say it?"

"Yes, he did. They may have been his last words."

"Pretty brave to stand up for our country that way," he said.

"Yes, it was," I agreed. "Now, let's get back to Abigail and Mercy.

"Mercy also wrote a response to the Boston Tea Party. In a letter to another friend, Hannah Winthrop, she said, 'The grandeur, magnificence and wealth of states seldom promoted either the virtue or happiness of individuals.'"

"What did she mean by that?" Hannah asked.

"That just because a government is big and rich doesn't mean that the people will be better off. She went on to say that England should stop controlling and profiting from the colonies.

"Abigail read everything that Mercy wrote, and she praised Mercy, in turn, for her bold positions on current events. For example, by the time they met, Mercy had already written her first play, *The Adulateur*, parts of which had been published in *The Massachusetts Spy*, a popular magazine that called for independence. Not long after, Abigail wrote to Mercy, 'I love the characters drawn by your pen.'"

"Did she see the play, Gomps?" Hannah asked.

"No, in those days, Puritans didn't attend plays or perform in them. They were only for reading."

"Why wouldn't Puritans act in a play?"

"Oh, that would have been blasphemy," I replied. "The Puritans believed that pretending to be someone else in public was ungodly."

"Wow, they were uptight!" Hannah said. "So, why write a play if you didn't believe it should be played?"

"To try to bring your story to life. Mercy hoped that people would 'get' the story as they read it. And, of course, her plays were performed by non-Puritans."

"So, what was the story?" Carter asked.

"It was a political satire of the British governor of Massachusetts and his henchmen. She gave everyone and everything funny names and told about their corruption and tyranny over the colony – in poetry."

"In poetry?" Hannah exclaimed.

"Yes, everything her characters said was in the form of a poem."

"Holy cow!" Hannah said. "How smart was she to think that up?"

"Well, to me, she's kind of like Shakespeare," I said. "That's how he wrote. And, those funny names she used were like those of Shakespeare, too."

"What's 'satire', Gomps?" Carter asked.

"Satire is making fun of something or someone. Mercy named the country 'Upper Servia'. She named the governor 'Rapatio' and his assistants were 'Meagre', 'Bagshot' and 'Captain Gripeall'.

"Ha, ha," Carter laughed. "Didn't she get in trouble?"

"Apparently not. Don't forget that she published everything anonymously until after the war. And, because she didn't use anyone's real name, the Governor had no proof that he was the target, or that she wrote it."

"Aha," he said. "Did she write any more plays?"

"Yes, she did. One year later, she released *The Defeat*, a continuation of *The Adulateur*. It was her first denunciation of the British maltreatment of the colonies. *The Defeat* was immediately published in the Boston Gazette and quickly became a rallying point for the opponents of British rule.

"Shortly after, Mercy wrote a letter to Catharine Macaulay, the English historian who promoted colonial independence. Macaulay was the one who had written to the Edenton Tea Party. In her letter, Mercy asked 'whether the genius of Liberty has entirely forsaken our devoted isle?' Macaulay wrote back that she hoped not, but that the recent actions of Parliament had given 'a complete answer.'"

"What did that mean?" Carter asked.

"Parliament's laws and taxes sent a message to the Colonies that England had no intention of allowing us to have freedom. As far as Macaulay was concerned, Parliament didn't need to say a word. What they did spoke for them."

"Got it," he said.

"Parliament's actions apparently spurred Mercy to take up her pen again," I continued. "She wrote another play, *The Group*, which criticized the latest actions of the Massachusetts Assembly, condemned the hardships that were imposed on wives in a man's world, and compared the oppression of the colonies by Parliament to that of women by men."

"Wow, tough stuff," Hannah said. "Independence of America and women. She took a chance there."

"She thought so, too," I said. "Afraid that she might have gone too far, Mercy wrote to Abigail that she might be condemned as blasphemous. Abigail wrote back that Mercy's writing was good for the colonies in that it promoted virtue and condemned vice.

"By this time, John Adams had gotten a copy of *The Group*, either from Abigail or from Mercy's husband. John wasted no time in getting the first two acts published in Philadelphia, in the *Boston Gazette*, and in the *Massachusetts Spy*. Three months later, the entire play was being sold on the streets of New York.

"While all this was going on, Mercy could not restrain herself from commenting further about the Boston Tea Party, and the boycott of British goods. She wrote a poem, 'The Squabble of the Sea Nymphs;

or the Sacrifice of the Tuscararoes,' in which she criticized the British in the strongest terms.

"Mercy sent the poem to Abigail, who passed it along to John. He had it published in the Boston Gazette and wrote to Mercy's husband, James, that her work was 'one of the uncontestable evidences of real genius.'

"In 1783 and 1785, after taking a break from publishing during the Revolutionary War, Mercy wrote her last two plays, *The Ladies of Castille* and *The Sack of Rome*. In both, she condemned the treatment of women and argued for their liberty as the equals of men. In *The Ladies of Castille*, she wrote:

> "Though weak compassion sinks the female mind,
>
> And our frail sex dissolve in pity's tears;
>
> Yet justice' sword can never be resheath'd
>
> 'Till Charles is taught to know we will be free;
>
> And learns the duty that a monarch owes,
>
> To Heaven-the people-and the rights of man."

"Who's Charles?" Carter asked.

"The King of England."

"What's it mean?"

"Here's what I think," I replied. "That treating women *as* the weaker sex may make them think they *are* weaker, but, once they become aware that they are equal, men in power can no longer keep them down."

"Works for me," Hannah said.

"Me, too," Carter said. "Amazing that she was arguing for women's rights so long ago."

"That's for sure," I said, "but there's more to Mercy's story."

"There's more?" Hannah asked.

"Yes, there is, maybe the most important part. It has to do with the ratification of the Constitution and the Bill of Rights.

"After the War, the Continental Congress learned that the Articles of Confederation hadn't worked. If you recall, the Articles failed because they didn't provide for any nationwide powers — what are called centralized powers. Each State was on its own.

"The Founders tossed out the Articles and started fresh. The result was the Constitution. It created centralized powers, but put checks and balances on them through the Separation of Powers, Limited Government, and States' Rights.

"When Mercy read the Constitution, she opposed it. To her, the centralized powers made it easy for the Federal Government to get too big and strong, like a monarchy. So, out came her pen.

"In 1788, Mercy wrote an essay titled 'Observations on the New Constitution, and on the Federal and State Conventions' and signed it 'The Columbia Patriot.' In that essay, she explained her opposition to the Constitution, as proposed. She felt that there should be protections *for* the people, in addition to the protections *against* the powerful and that was a Bill of Rights.

"Now, Elbridge Gerry, one of Mercy's old friends and a leading member of the Massachusetts and Continental Congresses, had publicly opposed the Constitution, too, and had refused to vote for it in the Massachusetts Ratifying Convention. He agreed with Mercy that there should be protections *for* the people and he made his opinions known.

"After Mercy's essay was published, many believed that Gerry wrote it, but documentary historians now know that it was Mercy. And it became the most important argument for a Bill of Rights in the Massachusetts Convention and in the nation."

"Why do you say, '. . . and in the nation', Gomps?" Hannah asked.

"Remember that Elbridge Gerry proposed a compromise that Massachusetts would ratify the Constitution if James Madison would offer a Bill of Rights to Congress after the Constitution had been voted in. Madison accepted the compromise."

"Why Madison, Gomps?" Hannah asked.

"He wrote the Constitution and spoke for the people who supported it.

"Massachusetts ratified the Constitution and the compromise was adopted by other States. Madison kept his promise and the States proceeded to ratify the Bill of Rights, too."

"Was the compromise a law, Gomps?" Carter asked.

"Nope, just what amounted to a handshake."

"That was a lotta trust," he continued.

"Yes, it was," I said, "but, in those days, your word was your bond."

"So, if it hadn't been for Mercy, the Constitution wouldn't have been approved?" Hannah asked.

"Quite possibly, Hannah, at least, not as quickly or in the way that it was."

"This time, *I* call Amazon," she said.

"For sure," I said, "and maybe a Founder."

"She wrote all those plays and poems," she continued. "Those had to have made a difference in how people felt."

"I'm sure you're right, Hannah, but that still wasn't all that she did. We'll come back to the rest next time. Right now, this story time has gone on long enough."

# 22

## CLASH OF TWO AMAZONS

"Tonight I'm going to tell you about the clash of the Amazons – Abigail Adams and Mercy Otis Warren," I began. "As relations between England and the Colonies became increasingly tense, Mercy continued to watch and document key events. Through her own eyewitness and in newspapers, handbills, and the eyewitness accounts of family, friends and messengers, Mercy became a virtual library of records.

"Finally, John Adams wrote to Mercy in January, 1776, suggesting a deal with her. He wrote that 'I will draw the character of every new personage I have an opportunity of knowing, on condition you will do the same.' She took the deal.

"Mercy became the central source of information for a wide range of people, including her husband, James, John Adams, Abigail, other Founders, and even for Catharine Macaulay, in England.

"In 1775, Mercy decided that she would write a history of the period. She called it, *History of the Rise, Progress and Termination of the American Revolution.*"

"How could she know at the time that there would be a Revolution?" Hannah asked.

"There was no way for her to know exactly, Hannah, but she sensed that big things were about to happen. In January, 1775, after Abigail had reported the quartering of British troops in Braintree homes, Mercy wrote back, '... the righteous cause in which the undaunted patriots of America have struggled for many years will finally succeed.' And a month later, she wrote, '. . . some of the worthiest . . . will fall in the conflict and perhaps the whole land be involved in blood.'"

"When did she write that?" Carter asked.

"Early 1775."

"Before the Declaration of Independence?"

"Eighteen months before."

"So she could see it coming," he continued.

"Yes, she could," I added. "What we're not sure of is when she decided to write the history. It had to be in 1775, because Abigail wrote in reply to one of Mercy's letters in late 1775 that she looked forward to reading her 'historic page.' In a return letter, Mercy asked her for every bit of information that came to her through newspapers, handbills, and flyers and even for '. . . part of certain private journals . . . [having] more about certain public characters [and events].'"

"Hold it, Gomps," Carter said. "What did she mean by 'private journals'? Abigail's? John's?"

"That's what I take it to mean. Who else's private journals would Abigail have access to? I think that Mercy was asking for personal, inside information."

"That's what it sounds like to me, too," he said. "That's asking a lot, even from a friend, isn't it?"

"Seems that way. And you need to keep that in mind, because this whole project blew up in Mercy's face many years later."

"Whoa, Gomps," Hannah exclaimed. "That sounds serious. What happened?"

"It *was* serious. Here's how it played out.

"Even six months before the Declaration, news was coming in to Mercy from many sources. She kept it, organized it and began to write.

"She continued to make vague references to her *History*, but showed her work to no one until twelve years later, in January, 1787, when she asked James Winthrop, the Harvard College Librarian, to review the first few chapters.

"Winthrop's review, sent to Mercy in a letter, was favorable and gave her the courage to publish it. She did so in 1805."

"Eighteen more years, Gomps?" Carter said. "It doesn't sound like she was encouraged."

"You wouldn't think so, but she wanted to add more to the book. By that time, the war was over. She had delayed its publication so she could cover the postwar period.

"Mercy was particularly intent on including John Adams's career. By that time, he had served as an ambassador in Europe, as Vice President under Washington, and as President for his one term."

"Got it," he said. "Makes sense."

"Mercy's *History* gained some acclaim," I continued, ". . . except with the Adamses."

"What do you mean, Gomps?" Hannah interrupted. "They were best friends!"

"Yes, the operative word is 'were,'" I said. "Mercy was never one to soften her thoughts, and she was not about to start for John. She described him and his roles in the new nation in what the Adamses considered unflattering terms.

"She criticized John for a number of things, including: that he let his prejudices get the better of his judgment; that he accomplished nothing as ambassador to England; that he was partial to a monarchy, in opposition to his stated beliefs in representative government; that he was cold, cranky, unpolished, and disliked. She criticized both his career and his character.

"It didn't help that the two families had strong differences in their political philosophies. Mercy had strong republican beliefs – that government should be representative of the people – while the Adamses believed that a strong central government was needed. So, what Mercy saw in John as overbearing and tyrannical, he and Abigail considered essential and justifiable."

"How did the Adamses react?" Hannah asked.

"At first, with silence. Mercy heard nothing from them for two years."

"Two years?" Carter asked.

"Two years. No visits, no letters, no messages through friends. Nothing.

"To other friends, Mercy worried that the Adamses might be sick (which to some extent they were), but otherwise didn't guess."

"Did she think it was because of her book?" Carter asked. "Did she think they might be mad?"

"I don't think so, Carter. She thought she had treated John fairly and heard nothing to the contrary. The reviews of her book were mixed, but there were no direct references to her comments about John. Even those reviews that were critical of her were refuted by later reviews, so I think she thought of the silence only as a mystery.

"On March 9, 1807 Mercy got a letter from Abigail. In it, Abigail reported a bout of sickness, but thanked Mercy for her last letter written in the fashion of their 'ancient friendship.' Abigail went on to hope that they might have a 'closer and more cordial union in the world of spirits to which we are hastening.'"

"Uh, oh," Hannah said. "Does that mean what I think it means?"

"What's that?" I replied.

"That they might be friends again in heaven," she said.

"That's how I interpreted it," I said. "It sounded ominous, didn't it?"

"Yah," Hannah said. "That wasn't good."

"Yes, and it doesn't appear that Mercy responded. There was silence again for the next four months.

"Finally, on July 11, John wrote a long letter to Mercy refuting her 'errors' about him, paragraph by paragraph. He wrote that he was correcting her 'in the spirit of friendship, that you may have an opportunity in the same spirit to correct.' Then he stated his objections in the strongest terms, backed up with citations of his achievements.

"'Never,' he insisted, 'had I ever acted out of passion or prejudice,' and challenged Mercy to cite examples. 'Absolute monarchy,' he said, 'was tyranny' which he had opposed his whole life, and he accused her of 'going the utmost length' to misrepresent his position. He went on like that for several pages, concluding, 'I wait with impatience your answer.'"

"Holy cow!" Carter said. "So much for that friendship. What did Mercy do?"

"John's letter surprised her. I think she was still expecting some kind of praise, even after Abigail's March letter. She got furious and wrote him back the same day, attacking both his criticisms and his character."

"She should have waited 'til the next day," Carter said. "Dad says it's always good to sleep on it. You might say something you are later sorry for."

"That would have been good advice," I said. "Too bad you weren't there to give it, because her letter just added fuel to the fire.

"Mercy wrote to John that his accusations must have resulted from his disappointment in the defeat of his political party in the last elections."

"Wahoo," Carter shouted, as he rolled backwards on the sofa. "He was taking out his election loss on her? That's what she accused him of? Oh, this is getting good!"

"Yes," I agreed, "she went on to defend her book in every respect, even in her criticism of his 'natural irritability of temper' as being an observation he should have welcomed."

"What an insult!" Hannah said. "And they had been friends for 30 years?"

"Not any more," I said. "This was just the beginning of ten letters from John over the next six weeks, detailing every slight, oversight and fault in her book, and six letters from Mercy, responding to them.

"The barrage ended with Mercy's last letter in which she agreed to consider his suggestions if she ever did a second edition. This was a false promise, since she was 79 years old by this time and had no intention of changing her book."

"What about Abigail?" Hannah asked. "Sounds like she was caught in the middle."

"Well, you could say that Abigail might have had to side with John because it was expected of a wife in those days," I replied, "but there was more to it than that.

"I think that Abigail was shocked at Mercy's character assassination of John. Mercy's charges of self-interest and greed as well as incompetence as an ambassador were in opposition to the man that Abigail knew. Abigail was liberal with her complaints to John about his habits, but these accusations were not among them.

"Also, Abigail was as fervent a believer in a strong central government as was John. They supported one another in this belief in letters exchanged over many years. So I think that the differences of opinion she had with Mercy on this would always put Abigail on John's side.

"And, there was one thing that Mercy let slip that may have turned Abigail against her. Mercy referred to John's 'natural irritability of temper' as a trait that Abigail herself had complained of. Now, maybe Abigail had talked in those terms with Mercy, but when I first read that my thoughts immediately went to Mercy's request of Abigail for their personal diaries — those 'certain private journals' — when she began to do her research for the book.

"If Abigail knew that she had brought those things up in casual conversation with her best friend, Mercy, she might well have felt hurt and angry. Had those private thoughts come from a diary, innocently shared, those feelings might have been turned to betrayal.

"In any event, the friendship lay in ruins. Their mutual friend Elbridge Gerry tried to get them to mend fences. In deference to him, Mercy wrote to Abigail in December of that year that it was possible to criticize one another's politics without it affecting their friendship. Abigail did not respond.

"The next year, Mercy's husband, James, died. This event would have been the one thing that might have prompted a friend to write a letter of condolence, if the friendship could have been salvaged.

"Abigail remained silent. Instead, she wrote to her daughter, saying that all the 'injustice' and 'bitterness' that had been exchanged with Mercy left her no choice but to refrain: 'I thought a letter of the kind would appear insincere.'

"Abigail and Mercy would not contact each other for another four years.

"Finally, in 1812, Abigail, her daughter Nabby and her granddaughter Caroline visited Mercy. The occasion was the aftermath of a physical attack on Congressman Charles Turner Jr. on Mercy's front door step. Turner was a member of Mercy's political party and was on his way to visit her when he was set upon by a gang of Federalists. Mercy got him inside, but he was badly injured.

"Abigail had heard about the assault and went to see Mercy a month later to see how she was doing. Mercy had suffered no injuries, but the emotional upset and the resulting court case gave Abigail concern for her old friend.

"The visit gave both women a chance to heal old wounds. They caught up on old news, carefully avoiding the subject of Mercy's book and their bitter exchanges over it. 'As a gesture of friendship,' Mercy gave Abigail a lock of her hair with the hope that the two families could put aside their differences.

"Mercy followed with a letter hoping for peace with John, too. That repair was still not to be. Elbridge Gerry, perhaps having been prompted by Mercy, visited the Adamses to see if he could continue the mending. He reported that Abigail told him that John 'did not regret this circumstance' of his estrangement from Mercy.

"Not one to give up easily, Elbridge tried one last time a few months later, and it worked. Abigail wrote to Mercy and included a handkerchief and a ring in which she had set a lock of her own hair interwoven with some of the hair that Mercy had sent her, as '. . . a token of love and friendship.' And with that, they picked up their correspondence again."

"Whew," Hannah said. "What a shame it would have been if they had stayed enemies."

"Yes," I said, "it would have been. Sadly, their reunification would never be complete.

"By that time, Mercy was showing her age – she was 84. And while her curiosity continued, her capacity for a new project was gone. Still, she kept up her correspondence with Abigail.

"Then tragedy struck – John and Abigail's daughter, Nabby, died. Mercy wrote them a letter of condolence, and, perhaps finally wanting bygones to be bygones, John wrote back to Mercy, thanking her for her sentiments and enclosing two old documents. One of them was a letter from the governor of Pennsylvania praising Mercy's brother, Jemmy, for his public speaking ability.

"That letter repaired the last link in the chain of correspondence between Mercy and the Adamses.

"Nine months later, Mercy was told that someone had claimed authorship of her play, *The Group*, in a display of the original document at the Boston Athenaeum. Infuriated, Mercy wrote to John, asking him to correct the claim, since he knew firsthand that she had written it.

"Sometime later, John did so, because he wrote to Mercy on August 17, 1814 that he had gone to the Athenaeum and had written a correction in the record, certifying that Mercy was the author."

"Did they ever meet in person again?" Carter asked.

"You mean after Abigail's visit in 1812?" I asked.

"Yeah."

"Apparently not," I said. "In July 1814, Mercy had invited the Adamses to her home in Plymouth for a visit, but there is no record of their having gone."

"That's too bad," he said.

"By this time, they were all quite frail," I said, "and it may be that John and Abigail felt that they just couldn't bear the travel."

"Well, he was at least strong enough to visit the Athenaeum," Carter countered.

"Hmm," I said, "yes, he was. What do you make of that?"

"Maybe the friendship was patched up to the writing level, but not the face-to-face level," he replied.

"Hannah, what do you think?" I asked.

"Makes sense," she replied. "John was sensitive to criticism, and the things she'd said about him were really bad."

"Beyond forgiveness?" I asked.

"Maybe if it was just once," she replied, "you know, something that slipped out, but she said things in the book and later in her letters. Once you say things like that, the other person will always remember."

"That's something for all of us to keep in mind," I said. "Now, let's see how this part of the story ended.

"A few months after getting John's letter about the Athenaeum, Mercy was entertaining friends for a few days and suddenly fell ill. She went to bed and seven days later, on October 19, 1814, she died."

"That was it?" Carter asked.

"Just about, Carter. She got up once to try to eat breakfast, but went right back to bed. She died quietly, at 87 years of age."

"Did the Adamses go to her funeral?" Carter asked.

"I was curious about that myself. I looked, but couldn't find any evidence of it."

"So maybe the wounds were never fully healed," Hannah said.

"It's possible," I said. "Something like that would be hard to forget, for both sides."

"Still, Mercy was important," Carter said. "She did so much. You have to put her with the top Amazons.

"Did the two families have anything to do with each other after she died?"

"It doesn't look like it. Mercy's husband, James, was dead, as was her brother Jemmy. Both Abigail and John were getting on in years, Mercy's favorite Adams child, Nabby, was dead, and Mercy had never struck up a friendship with their son, John Quincy. I don't think there was any common ground left."

"What happened to Abigail?" he continued.

"Well, to finish her story we need to go back several years," I said. "Next time."

# 23

## THE LAST OF THE AMAZONS

"Let's start with John Adams's whereabouts," I said. "Late in 1779, he traveled from Boston to Paris to start peace and commerce negotiations with England. In 1780, he was made minister to the Netherlands in order to negotiate a loan with the Dutch. Between France and the Netherlands, he stayed until 1785.

"As the years went by, Abigail became increasingly lonely for John's company. Letters were not enough, so she overcame her reluctance to cross the Atlantic and in 1784, she sailed with Nabby to meet John. The family settled in France while John was in the Netherlands and then joined him there.

"In 1785, John was named ambassador to England, and they moved to London. Abigail was relieved, since she had been uncomfortable with the French way of conducting diplomacy."

"Why was that, Gomps?" Hannah asked.

"Abigail had been told that French diplomats were arrogant, petty, scheming, and unfriendly. Even John had said so. Her living in France confirmed to her that the reports were true. Being plainspoken and direct, she never seemed able to adapt to these French statesmen for whom nuance was a way of life. So the move to London promised a more familiar lifestyle.

"Sadly, Abigail found life in the Royal Court of England to be just as discomforting – different, but unpleasant. Nonetheless, she did her duty as a diplomat's wife. Finally, John was summoned home in 1788 and her ordeal was over.

"During their last year in England, the Adams's friends in Massachusetts were making arrangements for their return. Principal among these was the negotiation for the purchase of a house that they had always wanted – the Vassall-Borland property.

"John and Abigail had admired Vassall-Borland, perhaps even coveted it, at least since 1782, when Nabby's suitor at the time, Royall Tyler, bought the place. An estate by Massachusetts standards, the property was 83 acres of rolling meadows in Braintree, surrounding a small mansion fitted out in mahogany paneling. Ownership had gone back to the original family, and while the Adamses were still in England, two of their friends negotiated the purchase for them.

"Upon their return to the United States, John and Abigail became property managers again. In addition to the newly acquired estate, they still owned the 'small house' and farm where John grew up, as well as the South Queen Street house in Boston. Before she left for Europe, Abigail had negotiated to have tenants occupy all of their properties. When they came back, she left those tenants in place, since the estate would be their new home.

"When John and Abigail took possession, Vassall-Borland was in rough shape. Undeterred, Abigail arranged for and supervised the renovations. She had a wing added, oversaw repairs, and took on its complete redecoration.

"From 1789 to 1818, life for Abigail was a series of nine relocations between Braintree, New York City, Philadelphia, Washington, DC, and, finally, back to Quincy for the last time until her death in the old house on October 28, 1818."

"Wow," Hannah said, "all that moving. That, in itself, took amazing strength. But, didn't you say that John was the Vice President *and* President?"

"I did."

"What did she do as his wife?" she asked.

"Not what you might think, Hannah. She took her role to be mostly ceremonial – at least in public.

"Right after John became Vice President, they moved into a New York City house called Richmond Hill. Big place with white columns. John had rented it soon after he was elected.

"Abigail supervised the move from Braintree and the setup of the household in New York. Richmond Hill was not in the best of shape, so she had to oversee repairs, as well.

"Abigail understood that she would be expected to entertain official visitors to the capital. She was in frequent contact with Martha Washington to plan for it. Once Martha had chosen Fridays as her regular time to entertain guests, Abigail settled on Mondays. She received visitors, hosted teas and held weekly dinners for twenty and more people.

"By herself?" Carter asked.

"No, she had a staff of 15 to help her run the house."

"But, she was in charge," he continued.

"Yes, she was, so she had to know what had to be done."

"Thought so," Carter concluded.

"Is that all she did, Gomps?" Hannah asked.

"No. Abigail couldn't keep herself from observing and commenting on the things that were going on around her. In letters to her friend, Mary Cranch, she described the impressive qualities of George and Martha Washington and their handling of events. When George Washington fell desperately ill with influenza, she wrote to her uncle, Dr. Cotton Tufts, that 'His death would have the most disastrous consequences.'"

"To the country?" Carter asked.

"Yes. She said, '. . . the union of the states, and consequently the permanency of the Government depend under Providence upon his Life.'"

"What did she mean by Providence, Gomps?" Hannah asked.

"God. She was saying that, in the end, the fate of Washington and of the country was in God's hands.

"At the same time, she understood that the future of the nation had to be forged by the people. One of her big worries was the money owed by the country from the war. She wrote again to Dr. Tufts later that year, '. . . I hope to see ways and means to pay all the State Debts,' but she wondered if the Legislature had the courage 'to take so decisive a step.'"

"Did they?" Carter asked.

"Yes, they did – in a curious way. Alexander Hamilton, Thomas Jefferson and James Madison agreed that the war debt would be taken on by the new government, if the national capital was moved to the South."

"Oh, yeah," he said. "You told us about that last year."

"That's right," I said, "but, they hadn't chosen the place, so they moved it to Philadelphia, first.

"Abigail knew that the capital would be moving to Philadelphia and that she would have to move the household once again. The announcement came on July 16, 1790 at a time when some of her tenants in Braintree were leaving and Abigail and some of her family had taken ill. It was not a good time, but she made the best of it.

"The Adams's Philadelphia house was called Bush Hill. Despite her own illness and that of other family members, Abigail began receiving visitors within days of their arrival.

"She was tough," Hannah said.

"Yes, she was."

"How'd she do it?"

"I think she was looking forward to going back home for a visit," I said. "The session of Congress would be over in March and she was planning to return to Braintree in May. There she would see to the tenancies of their properties, shore up the family finances, meet with relatives, and tend to her failing health."

"What was wrong with her?" Hannah asked.

"Over the years, she suffered from a variety of things. She had rheumatism-like symptoms, failing eyesight and on-and-off influenza. As she aged, these got worse.

"She stayed in Philadelphia only during sessions of Congress. In late 1791, even that infrequency was broken when she became too ill to accompany John for the next session. She would not return to Philadelphia for five years – all due to sickness.

"Neither did she spend much time with John when the capital moved to Washington, D.C. and they moved into the White House. During those last four years, Abigail lived in it for only 18 months. The rest of the time she was back in Braintree.

"Wherever she lived, though, Abigail continued to write to others about her interpretation of events. During this period, she wrote frequently to Jefferson, Elbridge Gerry, to the Cranches, to John, of course, and to other family members expressing her views on a wide range of policy and political issues.

"Going back to your observation, Hannah - yes, that was a lot of moving. But, it was just part of Abigail's productive life. In addition to the lifelong political consulting she did for John and many other Founders, she was a property manager, businesswoman, crusader for women's rights, and reporter. And she left behind a few surprises at her death in 1818 . . ."

"You've always got a surprise in your stories, Gomps," Carter said. "Just when we think you're all done, you spring another one on us. What is it this time?"

"I'll take that as a compliment," I said. "In her will, Abigail left to their son, John Quincy, a farm that had been left to her by her uncle Norton . . ."

"Wait, Gomps," Hannah interrupted. "What was that about?"

"The farm?"

"Yeah."

"I guess she was managing that, too, although it doesn't appear in her correspondence. That's not the only one, either. Her father had left to her a half interest in some other acreage. She left that to her son Thomas."

"Huh," she said.

"Wait, there's more," I said.

"This goes on and on," Carter said.

"Yeah, I guess it does, Carter. Abigail owned about 4,000 dollars' worth of corporate stock, and she had that sold and divided up among her surviving grandchildren and nieces and nephews. She apparently owned the Haverhill Bridge, too, and gave her shares in it to her granddaughters."

"Owned a bridge?" Hannah exclaimed.

"That's what her will said, and that wasn't the only one. She owned the Weymouth Bridge, too, and gave her shares in *that* to her sons. She gave her personal possessions, like jewelry and clothes, to various relatives and friends."

"Holy cow!" Hannah exclaimed. "That's a lotta stuff!"

"Yes, I was surprised, too," I said.

"She did OK," Hannah said.

"I think so," I said. "She's another example of the women who paid no attention to what they weren't supposed to be able to do."

"Does that mean it's over?" Carter asked.

"As far as the Amazons' stories, yes," I replied. "I tried to finish with what I think were the ones who were the strongest or had the most interesting stories, but Abigail and Mercy are the last of my Amazons."

"Were there more of them, Gomps?" Hannah asked.

"Amazons, you mean?"

"Yeah."

"I'm sure there were, Hannah, but these are the ones that I thought would be most interesting to you.

"No doubt there are others whose stories I just didn't come across; women who were Amazons, but maybe are unknown to historians or whose diaries haven't been published. And there were some women who did important things, but didn't come up to the level of Amazons."

"What did you consider an Amazon, Gomps?" Carter asked.

"The most important thing to me was achievement, accomplishment. It isn't enough that they thought something or said something. They had to have done something, whether it was write a book or run a business.

"The Founding was about building a nation, and there were plenty of women who helped lay the foundation through their deeds. That's the most important thing, and they make for the best and most inspiring stories."

"Gomps, wasn't it even harder for them than for the men?" Hannah asked.

"You mean to get things done?"

"Yeah."

"Absolutely. The Founders had to overcome the English traditions of social class and cultural limits, plus control by the King and Parliament. And they had the threat of being imprisoned or killed if they had been caught.

"These women faced all of that while breaking through the burdens on women as mothers and housekeepers and the laws of control by men. These Amazons didn't let any of that stop them.

"That's why I liked the petition by the Edenton Tea Party. Fifty-one women burned their tea, swore off English products and signed a petition that they had done it. And they called out the Sons of Liberty in Boston for having hidden behind costumes."

"Yeah, that was cool," Carter said. "Did they plan it like the Sons of Liberty did?"

"It doesn't look like it, Carter. It looks more like Penelope Barker had an idea, sent word to all her friends, and just did it. In fact, I think that may have been a difference between how the men and women did things. The men did a lot of planning. The women saw a need and went for it."

"Were there any similarities?" Carter asked.

"The most obvious one was that the Amazons came from all backgrounds, just like the men. Some came from the cities and some from the country; some came from wealth, and some were poor. And some were from the North and some from the South.

"But the most important similarity was education. One way or another, these women became educated, in most cases in defiance of tradition. Granted, fathers and husbands had a hand in it, but these women were determined to learn just as their brothers learned. And their educations enabled them to do what they did.

"From Elizabeth I through Abigail Adams, education made the difference. And, speaking of Abigail, you have to admire her courage, along with Mercy Otis Warren's, to stand up for the rights of women.

"Those two, plus Catharine Macaulay, the English historian with whom they corresponded, became the stepping stones on which the next generation of crusaders relied, starting with Mary Wollstonecraft,

"Who's that?" Hannah asked.

"Wollstonecraft was an English writer who published *A Vindication of the Rights of Woman* in 1792. She is probably the first woman writer/ philosopher to address women's rights extensively.

"Wollstonecraft lived from 1759 to 1797, dying in childbirth at 38. One of her main themes was that, if women appear to be inferior to men, it is only because of a lack of education. She argued that women who were educated were the equal of men. Some regard her as the one of the first feminists."

"After Anne Hutchinson, Mercy and Abigail, that is," Hannah said.

"Yes, after them, I think," I said. "And I think that wraps up our stories about the American Amazons. They were an amazin' bunch, and I'm glad you were with me as we talked about them."

"That was great, Gomps," Carter said. "I learned a lot more than I thought I would. I'm glad I stuck with it. I thought it would be boring, but it wasn't. Thank you."

"Yeah, Gomps, that *was* great," Hannah echoed. "I didn't realize how important women were to the Founding and what they had to go through to do their part. They laid the foundation for our country and for us women, that's for sure."

"What was the biggest thing you learned?" I asked.

"That women can do just about anything they set their minds to," Hannah replied. "And they do."

"Carter?" I asked.

"People were no different than they are now," he replied. "People may not have had technology back then, but they wanted the same things and fought to get them."

"Well, I couldn't have said it better," I said. "Mandy? Mark? Anything to add?"

"Not for me," Mark said, "except to say thank you for all that you did. I learned a lot, too."

"Same here, Dad," Mandy said. "I learned about women I didn't know existed and I learned more about those I had heard of. Anyone can get inspired to go for it after hearing about what those women did. Thank you so much."

"Thank you for listening," I said. "And Peach asked me to thank you, too, for your patience with her stories. It was our pleasure and privilege to pass them along and I hope you'll do the same when the time comes. And with that, I'll say good night."

"Good night, Gomps."

"Night."

"See you soon, Gomps."

"We love you."

# AUTHOR'S NOTE

Thanks for joining Gomps, Hannah and Carter on their journey into the history of colonial women. Did you enjoy it? Here's what you can do next:

If you loved the book and have a moment to spare, I would really appreciate your writing a short review for me in one or both of the following sites:

http://www.amazon.com/dp/1502821222.
https://www.goodreads.com/review/new/24600189-american-amazons.

To an author, word-of-mouth is crucial. Won't you tell a friend or two about how much you enjoyed my book?

You can also sign up to be notified of my next book, as well as pre-release specials and giveaways. Just send me an email at:

alexbugaeff@cox.net

WANT MORE OF GOMPS, HANNAH AND CARTER?

Try my first book in The Grandfather Series, *Pilgrims To Patriots, A Grandfather Tells The Story*. Available in ebook and print formats at:

http://www.amazon.com/dp/1478266848.

Thank you, Alex Bugaeff

# AFTERWORD

The idea for *American Amazons* came to me during the research and writing of my last book, *Pilgrims To Patriots, A Grandfather Tells The Story*. In the course of that research, I found stories of women who had done amazing things during this period . . . things that changed history.

Some of those stories, like those of Molly Pitcher and Elizabeth Key, fit into that book and I included them there. I have retold those stories here – adding details that enrich them – because they are so much a part of the fabric of women's part in our Founding.

Other women's stories were not critical to the *Pilgrims To Patriots* saga, but still cried out for telling. Even before I finished that first book, I knew I had to tell them. As I did further research, I came upon many more of these stories – some already familiar and many that are not. Even the familiar ones, though, are often told only as abbreviations, side notes or human interest stories.

As I delved deeper into their letters, journals, papers, and achievements, I began to understand the contributions that women had made to the Founding and its history. Not only did many of the women familiar to us do more than is generally known, but the "unknowns", the women "unrecognized" except almost as footnotes, added immensely to the picture.

With so many stories to choose from, a first task was to decide which ones to include and which to exclude. It came down to a singular criterion - women who had an impact on the Founding, who did things that made a difference.

Still, I lacked an identity, a motif. Then, I remembered the letter by Arthur Iredell about the Edenton Tea Party. He called those 51 women "Amazons" and right there, I had my theme; these were "American Amazons."

As these women's stories came to life for me, I looked for things that might explain their exceptionality and patterns began to appear. They all seemed to have physical and emotional stamina – what, ironically, used to be called "strong constitutions." Women like Molly Pitcher, Nancy Hart and Deborah Sampson were physically strong and were able to tough it out in their circumstances. Those like Anne Hutchinson, Elizabeth de Berdt Reed and Caty Greene had perseverance – were not easily dissuaded, wouldn't take "no" for an answer.

One element that doesn't appear to play into the equation is family size. One might think that women with large numbers of children would have a harder time doing more than maintaining their households and raising their families, but some of the "Amazons", including Ann Catherine Green and Eliza Hamilton, had large families. Even without household "help" of one kind or another, there were many women who excelled.

Of less importance, perhaps, is birth order. It appears that few "Amazons" were first or second born, the exceptions being Eliza Pinckney, Martha Washington and Mercy Otis Warren.

The most important factor no doubt was education. Almost all of the "Amazons" became educated in one way or another, or at least had a good grasp of the situations surrounding them and what they faced. In addition to our modern day understanding of its importance, this attribute was considered to be the most important by big thinkers of the time, such as Abigail and John Adams, Mercy Otis Warren and Catherine Macaulay. We know this because they wrote about it at length and they practiced what they preached, educating themselves and assuring that the other women in their lives became educated.

Finally, there was a factor that all seemed to have: they ignored convention. They paid no attention to what they were supposed to do and not do. They seemed to recognize when something needed to be done and they just went ahead and did it.

Some would say that they defied tradition, but that implies that they committed conscious acts against authority. This is no doubt true of some. Certainly, Abigail Adams and Mercy Otis Warren spelled out the need for civil disobedience that would become a hallmark of our culture. But, few others committed intentional acts of defiance, the exceptions perhaps being Penelope Barker and Hannah McDougall.

In the course of making my choices, I was reminded of a slogan of a popular athletic shoe manufacturer: "Just do it." That's what these women did: they just did it. No wondering, "Should I?" No planning to minimize risk. No hiding their identities, as the Edenton Tea Party participants chided the Boston Tea Party men for having done. No concern for what others would think. Something needed to be done and they didn't hesitate.

In some cases, it might be said that they got away with it. That, *because* they were women, no one thought they were capable of what they did. Certainly this was true in the cases of spies, such as Lydia Darragh and Nancy Hart, and it was likely that those spies were aware of how the enemy viewed them and took advantage of it.

In other cases, probably the large majority, such as the Molly Pitchers and the "Paul Reveres", they acted, perceptions be damned.

However we characterize these women, though, they all had one thing in common — they changed history by their actions. They gave our country a richer tradition and made our new nation a better place. We are indebted to them for it.

In addition to the importance of telling these women's stories, I wrote this book for the same reasons that I wrote the first book in this series: *Pilgrims To Patriots, A Grandfather Tells The Story*, namely that the history of our nation's Founding is not being told to the general public or taught in schools.

A recent experience is a perfect example. At an ancient fife and drum muster, I was sitting in my booth to sell my book when a twelve year old girl came up to my table. She asked what my book was. I answered, "History." She said, "I like history, but they don't teach it in my school." I asked, "What do they teach?" She said, "Social Studies." I asked, "What do they teach in Social Studies?" She said, "How to feel sorry for people."

She picked up my book, leafed through it, put it down, and left. Ten minutes later, she returned with the money, bought my book, I inscribed it for her, and she skipped away, book in hand.

For those familiar with *Pilgrims To Patriots*, the format for *American Amazons* is the same, hence *The Grandfather Series, #2*. In a series of story times, a grandfather sits down with his two grandchildren, only in this book he tells them the stories of colonial women who changed history. Although the grandchildren are one year older than in *Pilgrims To Patriots*, the simple language and dialogue are very much the same.

You may have noticed what appear to be misspellings in some of the quotations I inserted. Abigail Adams spelled it "Laidies" in her letter to John demanding fair treatment for women. Arthur Iredell spelled it "esteem'd" in the letter to his brother ridiculing the Edenton Tea Party. In each case of a direct quotation, I left the spelling and punctuation as the writer wrote it as long as the meaning could still be made out.

I had two purposes for doing so. First, I wanted to maintain the feeling of the language of the time. And, second, I wanted to show that the English language differed slightly among the people. These differences showed the need for uniformity, but that was not to come until 1828 with the publication of Noah Webster's dictionary. Nonetheless, the colonists took care to make their thoughts clear.

I wrote *American Amazons* to stand on its own, although *Pilgrims To Patriots* is a foundation for it in many ways. You have discovered in the first few chapters that there is linkage between two, both in style and in the history itself. I have tried to bring the reader up to speed on the essentials in order to understand fully what I aim to say, but to get a complete picture, I recommend reading *Pilgrims To Patriots*, too.

As with the first book, I intend that parents, grandparents, children, and grandchildren read this book. I also recommend that parents and grandparents read it to the children.

Finally, I wrote this book for all those who have an interest in the history of colonial women. It turns out that there is far less research and far fewer publications on this subject than one might think and I hope that *American Amazons* can help in some small way to stimulate more of both.

Alex Bugaeff

Stafford Springs, Connecticut

# LEARN MORE

As this is the second book in The Grandfather Series, the same Learn More principles apply with this one as for the first. So, I have repeated the discussion of primary and secondary sources and of publication formats.

Similarly, the sources of primary materials remain much the same, both in print and online. Accordingly, I have repeated those citations here, as well – deleting those that have no bearing and adding those which add to the *American Amazons* database. You will find few deletions of this material, though, since references to women of the period are often found throughout.

I used the same approach with regard to the secondary materials: most history books of the period, though concentrating perhaps on the Founding men, have included substantial references to the women who are part of the stories being told.

A major difference between the histories of the Founding men and of the American Amazons is that there is far less material about the women than the men. This difference applies to both the primary and secondary material. Fewer women wrote about their experiences or had such writings saved when they did.

In addition, fewer historians have chosen to tell the stories of women of the period. For example, the papers of Alexander Hamilton and James Madison were conserved and published soon after their deaths

(by their wives), but the first major work about women of the period –
*The Women of the American Revolution* – wasn't published until 1848 (more
about that book later in this section).

I hope that reading this book about American Amazons has made
you want to learn more. Rather than list the many books, articles, journals, and letters that I studied for this book, I thought it would be more
helpful to limit the list to the ones that might be the most interesting.
These fall into two types: original or primary sources, and interpretations of primary sources, also known as secondary sources.

Original or primary sources are documents that the subjects themselves wrote. These include diaries, letters, journals, essays, books, and
more. Many of the writings of Abigail Adams, for example, exist in
their original forms or as copies, and are, therefore, primary sources.
We are lucky that the writings of some of the subjects in this book have
survived the centuries.

Interpretations or secondary sources are, for all practical purposes,
history books and articles. This book is a secondary source. Secondary
sources are written by people who study primary sources (and other
secondary sources, for that matter) and quote or interpret them in telling the story.

Any truth about a historical subject is more likely to come from the
person who wrote or said it than it is to come from a person who inter-
prets it. So it's often better to read a primary source. The problem with
primary source material from early American men, for historians and
casual readers alike, is that there is so much of it. George Washington's
writings alone take up more than 90 volumes. This is a good problem
to have. As said above, however, there is far less primary source material
by and about women.

Nonetheless, anyone, be it a historian or an interested general reader, must limit the amount of primary source information that they choose to include in their studies of any historical subject. What they include and exclude depends on a number of things: their choices of topic; why they are reading in that topic area or what readers they are writing for; their reasons for reading or writing that work; and their personal filters or biases. If you have not already, you may see some of my choices (as best I know them) in the Afterword to this book.

Primary Sources – See For Yourself

One of my mottoes has always been, "See for yourself." This probably came from my early years in the study of science. In science, nothing is taken for granted. Hypotheses are only "confirmed" (or not) by findings. Nothing is "proven, once and for all." To attempt to confirm a hypothesis, all students run experiments to see for themselves if they get the same results that others have.

The best way to be sure of historical accuracy is to "see for yourself." If you wonder whether something in this or any other book of history is true, look it up. Don't necessarily take anybody's word for it, including mine. That's what I did in my studies of early American history: I got things from the horses' mouths, as much as possible.

To help you to do that, I have listed below the most interesting primary sources (to me). Most are published and can be purchased. Most are now also online. Virtually all can be borrowed at a library. A few must be seen at the Library of Congress. See for yourself.

National Archives: Direct access to all primary sources held by the National Archives and available on-line. Also known as the "Rotunda." http://www.archives.gov/museum/visit/rotunda.html.

On-Line Library of Liberty: Look here first if you want direct access. Most of the primary sources used are carried here, as in a clearinghouse.

http://oll.libertyfund.org/#founders.

Search for biographical information:

http://www.biography.com/people.

Short essays on historical subjects:

http://www.earlyamerica.com/review.html.

North Carolina:

http://www.learnnc.org/lp/pages/4305

Roger Williams:

https://www.au.org/church-state/april-2003-church-state/featured/the-forgotten-founder

Anne Hutchinson:

http://historicbaptist.org/pastorsdocs/.

Abigail Adams:

http:/www.masshist.org/digitaladams/archive.

Mercy Otis Warren:

http://www.masshist.org/collection-guides/view/fa0235.

For hard-to-find people:

http://massachusetts.lostsoulsgenealogy.com.html.

http://www.bartleby.com.

Mary Alexander:

http://blog.nyhistory.org/fabric-samples-from-an-early-new-york-businesswoman

Eliza Pinckney:

http://indigobluesc.com/2010/06/25/notable-south-carolinians-eliza-lucas-pinckney

Catharine Greene: http://www.georgiaencyclopedia.org/articles/history-archaeology/catharine-greene-1755-1814.

http://msa.maryland.gov/msa/educ/exhibits/womenshall/html/green.html

Deborah Sampson: http://www.distinguishedwomen.com/biographies/sampson.html.

Grace and Rachel Martin: http://americanrevolution.org/women/women24.html.

The following are references for information about some of the women and men described:

Abigail and John Adams, *My Dearest Friend – Letters of Abigail and John Adams*, Margaret A. Hogan and C. James Taylor, eds. (Cambridge, MA, The Belknap Press of Harvard University Press, 2007).

George Washington, *The Writings of George Washington*, John C. Fitzpatrick, ed. (Washington: U.S. Government Printing Office, 1944), 39 vols. The full text is online at http://etext.virginia.edu/washington/fitzpatrick. Also, the University of Virginia has an edition of *The Papers of George Washington* — his diaries, his correspondence including letters to and from him, and other documents and maps — in progress: http://gwpapers.virginia.edu/project/index.html. You can browse this collection (read George Washington's diary!) through the Mount Vernon website: http://rotunda.upress.virginia.edu/founders/GEWN.xqy

Benjamin Franklin, *The Papers of Benjamin Franklin*. Yale University has been working on this scholarly edition of Franklin's voluminous writings since 1954, and it has now reached 40 volumes, which are published in physical book form by Yale University Press, at least some of which your local library may have. You can also browse and search the complete papers online for free: http://franklinpapers.org/franklin/. Start with this introductory essay which will walk you through Franklin's life, with links to many of his writings. http://franklinpapers.org/franklin/framedMorgan.jsp.

John Adams, *The Works of John Adams, Second President of the United States: with a Life of the Author, Notes and Illustrations, by his Grandson Charles Francis Adams* (Boston: Little, Brown and Co., 1856). Charles Francis Adams, ed. (Boston: Little, Brown & Co., 1856), 10 volumes. All online at the Online Library of Liberty: http://oll.libertyfund.org/2098

Alexander Hamilton, *The Works of Alexander Hamilton* (Federal Edition), Henry Cabot Lodge, ed. (New York: G.P. Putnam's Sons, 1904), 12 vols. Online at the Online Library of Liberty: http://oll.libertyfund.org/title/1712.

Thomas Jefferson, *The Writings of Thomas Jefferson*, Albert Ellery Bergh, ed. (Washington: The Thomas Jefferson Memorial Association of the United States, 1907), 20 vols. Online at http://www.constitution. org/tj/jeff.htm. Another edition, *The Works of Thomas Jefferson*, Federal Edition, Paul Leicester Ford, ed. (New York and London, G.P. Putnam's Sons, 1904-5). 12 vols., is available at the Online Library of Liberty, http://oll.libertyfund.org/1734.

James Madison, *The Writings of James Madison*, Gaillard Hunt, ed. (New York: G. P. Putnam's Sons, 1900), 9 vols. Online at the Online Library of Liberty, http://oll.libertyfund.org/title/1933

William Bradford, *Of Plymouth Plantation, 1620-1647*, Samuel Eliot Morison, ed. (New York: Alfred A. Knopf, 2004). There are several editions out there. Morison has written an excellent introduction, and I recommend his version.

John Winthrop, *The Journal of John Winthrop, 1630-1649*, Richard S. Dunn, James Savage, and Laetitia Yeandle, eds. (Cambridge, MA: Harvard University Press, 1996).

*The Constitution of the United States with the Declaration of Independence and the Articles of Confederation*, R.B. Bernstein, introduction (New York: Fall River Press, 2002). This is a pocket-size edition that includes all of the Amendments with an excellent introduction and timeline. The texts of all three add up to less than 80 pages. Read them.

Alexander Hamilton, James Madison, John Jay, *The Federalist*, Benjamin F. Wright, ed., (Cambridge, MA: Belknap Press of Harvard University Press, 1961; New York: Barnes & Noble Books, 2004). The 2004 edition has the subtitle *The Famous Papers on the Principles of*

*American Government.* Wright has compiled these 85 "letters to the editor" (also known as *The Federalist Papers*) brilliantly. He maintained their 18th Century writing style, but the arguments shine through.

❧

Secondary Sources

Why do people write history? We trust that they love the period and the subjects about which they write. Writing history honestly requires virtual obsession and unending hard work. Scholars bear the additional burden of "publish or perish." Most, if not all, hope that they earn money from book sales. Some may seek acclaim, although writing history may be one of the least likely roads to it. Some hope to interpret and present history so as to influence social trends.

So, writers of history read primary documents and the writings of others, sort out the story they want to tell and write it. Consciously or subconsciously, the personal baggage they bring to their writing finds its way into their writing. I'm no different.

For the reader and student of history, the question arises, "What is true?" That you have to figure out for yourself. Some writing is very persuasive. That is why primary sources are so important, but any one source may not be enough. There is evidence that, in retirement, James Madison rewrote or revised many of his papers because he wanted to improve or strengthen how he would be remembered.

The best single piece of advice is to read a lot on the period or subject that interests you. Read different authors' versions. Read about related periods or subjects that bear on your favorites. Read. As you go, a clearer picture will begin to form and you will be able to separate the wheat from the chaff.

There are a few dead giveaways, though, that an author is trying not only to paint a picture of what happened, but to tell you what you should think about it. If an author uses words such as "What other conclusion is there?" a warning light should go on in your brain — a signal to seriously think about what other conclusions there indeed might be, and not just allow the author to persuade you.

If the author writes of a historical personage, "He would have said or done such and such (or worse yet, "thought such and such" or "felt such and such"), that is fiction, not history. The author doesn't have evidence on which to base the statement. The author may just be trying to liven up the narrative — responsible historians will tell you when they are imagining a scene or speculating about a character's thoughts — or, more dangerously, he or she may be using a historical figure as a mouthpiece to promote the author's point of view.

I used such a method in this book. For example, Peach came to the conclusion that General Gates must have known that his wife "spilled the beans", but that he forgave her because he loved her. The evidence, to Peach, was that they lived together afterward in London for many years, even having more children. In this instance, I tried to make clear that I was not citing this as historical "fact", but rather as a conclusion. If I failed, I offer my apologies. I had no intention of trying to promote a biased point of view.

A special word about television and film: beware. Both are produced primarily to earn money through entertainment (and to some extent to educate and influence broad groups of people). If the ratings are low or the box office is not there, they fail. So producers plan their productions for high ratings or box-office receipts. General story lines are filled in with what they want or what they think the viewer wants the history to have been, and historical honesty is left at the wayside if it might discourage viewership.

Here are books on early American figures that are worth reading – first, on women, then on men. There are many others, some perhaps more worthy. Some are recent; some less so. Some are more "scholarly"; some less so. All would be good additions to your learning and to your library.

Elizabeth F. Ellet, *The Women of the American Revolution*, 3 vols. (New York, NY: Baker and Scribner, 1849). The first known comprehensive history of women in early America. Much of the reference material comes from interviews of the subjects and/or their family members, plus primary documents in their original forms, often provided by the subjects or family. Ellet is a fascinating historical character in her own right and writes in a conversational style typical of the period. This work is probably the foundation on which other histories of women of the period have been written.

Phyllis Lee Levin, *Abigail Adams, A Biography,* (New York, NY, Thomas Dunne Books St. Martin's Griffin, 1987). A comprehensive work in a traditional history writing style. Levin illustrates her observations about Abigail with extensive quotations from her letters and journals.

Cokie Roberts, *Founding Mothers: The Women Who Raised Our Nation* (New York, NY, Harper Collins, 2004). Roberts liberally sprinkles her comments and opinions through asides to the reader. She leaves no doubt about her position on women of the period, but she does it with a breezy, conversational style.

Nancy Rubin Stuart, *The Muse of the Revolution: The Secret Pen of Mercy Otis Warren and the Founding of a Nation,* (Boston, MA, Beacon Press, 2008). Outstanding blend of scholarship and readability concerning this little-known woman who was critical to the Founding.

Lynne Withey, *Dearest Friend, A Life of Abigail Adams* (New York, NY, The Free Press, 1981). Tends more toward the social and cultural, including Abigail's upbringing and family life – subjects worthy of treatment, nonetheless. Withey tells Abigail's story in a readable and enjoyable fashion.

Andrew M. Allison, Jay A. Parry and W. Cleon Skousen, *The Real George Washington: The True Story of America's Most Indispensable Man* (Malta, ID: National Center for Constitutional Studies, 1991 and 2008). Easy reading. Includes over 200 pages of quotations from Washington's writings on a wide range of subjects, grouped by subject. This is volume 3 of the publisher's American Classic Series.

Andrew M. Allison, W. Cleon Skousen and M. Richard Maxfield, *The Real Benjamin Franklin: The True Story of America's Greatest Diplomat* (Malta, ID: National Center for Constitutional Studies, 1982 and 2008). Easy reading. Includes over 200 pages of quotations from Franklin's writings on a wide range of subjects, grouped by subject. This is volume 2 of the publisher's American Classic Series.

Andrew M. Allison, M. Richard Maxfield, K. DeLynn Cook, and W. Cleon Skousen, *The Real Thomas Jefferson The True Story of America's Philosopher of Freedom,* 2nd ed. (Malta, ID: National Center for Constitutional Studies, 1983 and 2008). Easy reading. Includes over 200 pages of quotations from Jefferson's writings on a wide range of subjects, grouped by subject. This is volume I of the publisher's American Classic Series.

Francis J. Bremer, *John Winthrop: America's Forgotten Founding Father* (New York, Oxford University Press, 2003).

Carl Van Doren, *Benjamin Franklin* (New York: Viking Press, 1938; PenguinBooks, 1991). This is a rigorously researched and written book in the tradition of the 19ᵗʰ Century historical scholars. It is heavy going, but the writing is supported by extensive quotes from Franklin's works. Your effort will be rewarded.

David McCullough, *John Adams* (New York: Simon & Schuster, 2001). As good a combination of serious history and storytelling as you will find. McCullough brings Adams to life as no one has before. Weaves Abigail into the story extensively. He has received well-deserved recognition for this work.

Ron Chernow, *Alexander Hamilton* (New York: Penguin Press, 2004). A clear and complete biography, this book raises Hamilton to a deserved level. Chernow blends Hamilton's words with those of his contemporaries into a rich and vivid portrait of the man and his times.

Ralph Ketcham, *James Madison: A Biography* (Charlottesville, VA: The University Press of Virginia, 1990). Generally recognized to be the preeminent work on Madison. This is a scholarly tour de force covering his entire life in detail, including many of Dolley's achievements.

Richard Labunski, *James Madison and the Struggle for the Bill of Rights* (New York: Oxford University Press, 2006). Labunski deftly weaves together Madison's leadership and the story of the development of the Bill of Rights. Sadly, he omitted the extent of the contribution that Mercy Otis Warren made to the ratification debate.

# ABOUT THE AUTHOR

Alex Bugaeff is the award-winning author of *Pilgrims to Patriots: A Grandfather Tells the Story*. The first book in the Grandfather series, it won honorable mention at the New York Book Festival in 2013.

The author continues this highly original series with a new focus on American women, *American Amazons: Colonial Women Who Changed History*.

Bugaeff has a master's degree in public administration and a bachelor's degree in political science from the University of California, Berkeley. He's served as a research assistant in American political history at Berkeley, and has spent thirty years consulting on domestic and international government relations. He's written over one hundred books and technical manuals for private clients. As a research historian, he focuses on early American governmental and cultural history, and relies on primary sources such as letters and diaries.

Bugaeff is married and has two children and two grandchildren. He currently lives in Connecticut.

# ABOUT THE TYPE

*A*merican Amazons was set in Centaur MT, 13 point. Centaur lends a
nobility and power to an easy-to-read typeface, thus befitting colonial times. Designed in 1912 by Bruce Rogers for the Metropolitan
Museum of Art, Centaur traces its roots to the 1469 Eusebius typeface
by Nicholas Jenson of Venice, Italy.

# THANK YOU

This book is the result of guidance and support from many people. Without their efforts, I would not have been able to bring it to fruition.

One of the most important things that a person can do for a writer is to tell them the truth about their book. All who helped me did that without reservation and I appreciate their honesty.

First, I thank my editor, Annie Gottlieb of New York City, for her expert and enthusiastic work on my manuscript. As with *Pilgrims To Patriots*, she understood the project and applied her considerable abilities to it. She again steered me with an experienced hand, helping me not to get too carried away.

I prevailed upon three special people to read my manuscript and to give me feedback. Of particular help was David Kapp – a dear friend and skilled editor in his own right. David spent far more time and effort with it than I expected and his input made it a much better book.

My loving daughter, Mandy, again took time from her busy schedule to read it and give me feedback. She made key observations that proved invaluable. I thank her for her direct and forthright thoughts.

Finally, I thank my wife, Pinny. She again played an essential role. In the midst of writing her own book, she always made time to listen, guide, suggest, and console. She is my cheerleader, confidant and sage.

In addition, she also made time to read my manuscript and give me her editorial assistance and honest opinion and suggestions. As with *PTP*, I am in her debt in ways too numerous to count.

I cannot close without recognizing my son, Gregor, for the love and support I needed, even when he was immersed in his sculpture. He was always encouraging, always there for me with a "Semper Fi." His steadfast belief in me was more important than he knew and his artistic input on the "look" of the book was invaluable.

After all the input I got along the way, it was still my responsibility to decide what to write and not to write. I am most appreciative for all the help I got, but in the end, any and all omissions, factual errors and errors in interpretation are mine alone.

Made in the USA
Middletown, DE
24 July 2015